Lecture Notes in Computer Science 17125

The series Lecture Notes in Computer Science (LNCS), including its subseries Lecture Notes in Artificial Intelligence (LNAI) and Lecture Notes in Bioinformatics (LNBI), has established itself as a medium for the publication of new developments in computer science and information technology research, teaching, and education.

LNCS enjoys close cooperation with the computer science R & D community, the series counts many renowned academics among its volume editors and paper authors, and collaborates with prestigious societies. Its mission is to serve this international community by providing an invaluable service, mainly focused on the publication of conference and workshop proceedings and postproceedings. LNCS commenced publication in 1973.

Peter Fettke · Iris Reinhartz-Berger ·
Joerg Evermann · Jeffrey Parsons
Editors

Advances in Conceptual Modeling

ER 2026 Workshops
CMLS, LLM4Modeling
St. John's, NL, Canada, October 5–8, 2026, Proceedings

Springer

Editors
Peter Fettke
German Research Center for Artificial Intelligence (DFKI) and Saarland University
Saarbrücken, Germany

Joerg Evermann
Memorial University of Newfoundland
St. John's, NB, Canada

Iris Reinhartz-Berger
University of Haifa
Haifa, Israel

Jeffrey Parsons
Memorial University of Newfoundland
St. John's, NB, Canada

ISSN 0302-9743 ISSN 1611-3349 (electronic)
Lecture Notes in Computer Science
ISBN 978-3-032-40376-6 ISBN 978-3-032-40377-3 (eBook)
https://doi.org/10.1007/978-3-032-40377-3

This Springer imprint is published by the registered company Springer Nature Switzerland AG
The registered company address is: Gewerbestrasse 11, 6330 Cham, Switzerland

Preface

This volume contains the proceedings of the workshops held at the 45th International Conference on Conceptual Modeling (ER 2026), hosted in St. John's, Canada. Since their introduction, workshops have provided an opportunity within the ER conference to present and discuss emerging ideas, concepts, and methods. They offer a setting for exchanging perspectives, exploring new directions, and discussing ongoing research. The workshops complement the main conference program by providing space for focused discussion of topics of interest to the conceptual modeling community and their applications in different domains.

Two workshops were organized at ER 2026. These were:

- 6th International Workshop on Conceptual Modeling for Life Sciences (CMLS)
- 4th International Workshop on Modeling in the Age of Large Language Models (LLM4Modeling)

Together, these workshops cover complementary topics within the broader area of conceptual modeling. CMLS and LLM4Modeling have a more applied focus, respectively addressing domain-driven modeling in the life sciences and the adoption and impact of transformative tools (large language models) in modeling.

Both workshops had independent program committees chosen by their organizers. Submissions were carefully reviewed by at least three members of the respective committee. Of the 9 submissions received, 5 research papers were accepted, corresponding to an overall acceptance rate of 56%. The accepted contributions address a range of topics and perspectives reflecting the themes and scope of the two workshops.

We are grateful to the general and program conference chairs for their support and advice. We would like to thank the workshop organizers for proposing, managing, and organizing the workshops, and for their efforts in bringing together these focused research discussions. Our thanks also go to the program committee members for reviewing the submissions and providing constructive feedback to the authors. Finally, we hope that the work presented in these proceedings will serve as a valuable reference for researchers and practitioners interested in the topics addressed by the workshops and will inspire further advances within the conceptual modeling community.

October 2026

Peter Fettke
Iris Reinhartz-Berger
Joerg Evermann
Jeffrey Parsons

Organization

Conference General Co-chairs

Jeffrey Parsons	Memorial University of Newfoundland, Canada
Joerg Evermann	Memorial University of Newfoundland, Canada

Program Committee Co-chairs

Anna Bernasconi	Politecnico di Milano, Italy
Marta Indulska	University of Queensland, Australia
Sudha Ram	University of Arizona, USA

Workshop Co-chairs

Peter Fettke	Saarland University and German Research Center for Artificial Intelligence (DFKI), Germany
Iris Reinhartz-Berger	University of Haifa, Israel

Posters and Demos Chairs

Roman Lukyanenko	University of Virginia, USA
Anna Wiedemann	Bern University of Applied Sciences, Switzerland

Tutorial Chairs

Steve Liddle	Brigham Young University, USA
Isabelle Wattiau	ESSEC Business School, France

Panel Chairs

Oscar Pastor	Universitat Politècnica de València, Spain
Veda Storey	Georgia State University, USA

Doctoral Consortium Chairs

Sotirios Liaskos	York University, Canada
Jolita Ralyté	University of Geneva, Switzerland

CEUR Proceedings Chair

Cesar H. Bernabe	University of Illinois Urbana-Champaign, USA

Publicity Chair

Shawn Ogunseye	Bentley University, USA

Proceedings Chairs

Matteo Mantovani	University of Verona, Italy
Alberto Garcia	Universitat Politècnica de València, Spain

CMLS

7th International Workshop on Conceptual Modeling for Life Sciences

Recent advances in understanding human conditions and diseases have opened new opportunities for their prevention, diagnosis, and treatment. The exponential growth of information in this field directly impacts the design and development of information systems, highlighting the need for novel approaches to processing healthcare data and knowledge.

The 7th International Workshop on Conceptual Modeling in Life Sciences (CMLS) was held as part of the ER 2026 conference. This workshop continues to be a meeting point for Information Systems (IS), Conceptual Modeling (CM), Data Management (DM), and Artificial Intelligence (AI) researchers working on healthcare and life science problems. It is also an opportunity to share, discuss, and find new approaches to improve promising fields, with a special focus on Genomic Data Management and Precision Medicine.

From the precise ontological characterization of complex biological systems to the modeling of operational processes and the development of decision-support methods for disease diagnosis and prevention, the research communities of IS, CM, DM, and AI play important roles. They can help to provide feasible, high-quality solutions for better healthcare.

CMLS aims to be a forum for discussing the conceptual modeling community's responsibility in supporting the life sciences in light of these new realities. We hope that the ideas presented will inspire further research and collaborations in these critical areas

Acknowledgements. The organizers express their gratitude to the authors, members of the program committee, organizers of ER 2026, and the invited speaker for their valuable contributions to the success of CMLS 2026. This workshop was supported by the VRAIN Research Center at Politècnica de València and was funded by the European Union under the BETTER project https://www.better-health-project.eu/, funded by the European Union's Horizon Europe research and innovation programme under grant agreement No. 101136262, and the UNICA project https://www.unica-project.eu/, funded by the European Union's Horizon Europe research and innovation programme under grant agreement No. 101218966. Alberto García was supported by the Universitat Politècnica de València through grant PAID-06-24.

October 2026

Alberto García S.
José Reyes
Nelly Barret
Carla Taramasco
Mireia Costa

Organization

Workshop Chairs

Alberto Garcá S.	Universitat Politècnica de València, Spain
José Reyes	Universitat Politècnica de València, Spain
Nelly Barret	INSA Lyon, CNRS LIRIS, France
Carla Taramasco	Universidad Andrés Bello, Chile
Mireia Costa	Universitat Politècnica de València, Spain

Program Committee

Anna Bernasconi	Politecnico di Milano, Italy
Stefano Ceri	Politecnico di Milano, Italy
Stefano Cirillo	Università degli Studi di Salerno, Italy
Nelly Condori	Universidad de Santiago de Compostela, Spain
Giovanni Giachetti	Polytechnic University of Valencia, Spain
Francesco Invernici	Politecnico di Milano, Italy
Carlos Íñiguez	Escuela Politécnica Nacional, Ecuador
Alberto H. F. Laender	Universidade Federal de Minas Gerais, Brazil
Madhulika Mohanty	Inria and Institut Polytechnique de Paris, France
Oscar Pastor	Universitat Politècnica de València, Spain
José Palazzo M. de Oliveira	Universidade Federal do Río Grande do Sul, Brazil
Ignacio Panach	University of Valencia, Spain
Pietro Pinoli	Politecnico di Milano, Italy
Edelweis Rohrer	Universidad de la República, Uruguay
Veda Storey	Georgia State University, USA
Juan Carlos Trujillo	University of Alicante, Spain

LLM4Modeling

4th International Workshop on Modeling in the Age of Large Language Models (LLM4Modeling)

Large language models (LLMs) are one of the most discussed topics today. They promise disruptive potential in many disciplines, including conceptual modeling. By now, it is well known that LLMs have the potential to create, analyze, and execute conceptual models in various formats and with varying reliability. Given the rapid pace of LLM development and its ever-improving capabilities, the future at the intersection of conceptual modeling and LLMs is uncertain yet full of opportunities. This leads to fundamental questions such as: How will the discipline of conceptual modeling deal with LLMs in the future? What influence will LLM have on modeling? How will the tasks of modeling change? Will modeling lose its importance? Or, the other way around, will modeling increase in importance in the future?

The workshop served as an established forum for discussions on the use of LLMs in the context of conceptual modeling. Here, we report on the fourth installment of the Workshop on Modeling in the Age of Large Language Models (LLM4Modeling), which took place at ER 2026 after it was originally established at the Modellierung 2024 conference in Potsdam, Germany.

A total of five papers were submitted. Through a rigorous review process, three papers were selected for presentation at the conference and publication in the proceedings. Each paper received three expert reviews in a double-blind review process.

In "Copy That? The Influence of Process Model Representation Format on LLM Comprehension," the authors conduct a systematic evaluation of the capability of LLMs to comprehend BPMN models in different representations.

The paper "Formalization Matters: Conceptual Modeling with Large Language Models in High-, Semi- and Low-Formal Tasks" explores the influence of differing degrees of formality of modeling tasks on the quality of an LLM's output.

In "From Text to Knowledge: An Ontology-Aware Triple Extraction Framework with LLMs," an approach for constructing knowledge graphs from textual descriptions with ontology-guided refinement cycles is presented.

Acknowledgments. Our gratitude is extended to everyone involved in making the fourth LLM4Modeling Workshop a success: the authors of all papers, the Program Committee members and additional reviewers for reviewing each paper, and the speakers who shared their valuable work. We would also like to thank the ER 2026 chairs and organizers for their support in preparing the workshop.

Hans-Georg Fill
Peter Fettke
Julius Köpke
Simon Curty

LLM4Modeling Organization

Program Chairs

Hans-Georg Fill	University of Fribourg, Switzerland
Peter Fettke	Saarland University and German Research Center for Artificial Intelligence (DFKI), Germany
Julius Köpke	University of Klagenfurt, Austria
Simon Curty	University of Fribourg, Switzerland

Program Committee

Dominik Bork	Vienna University of Technology, Austria
Robert Andrei Buchmann	Babeş-Bolyai University of Cluj Napoca, Romania
Joerg Evermann	Memorial University of Newfoundland, Canada
Manfred Jeusfeld	University of Skövde, Sweden
Sanaz Saki Norouzi	Kansas State University, USA
Oscar Pastor	Universidad Politécnica de Valencia, Spain
Dimitris Plexousakis	FORTH Institute of Computer Science, Greece
Reinhard Schütte	University of Duisburg-Essen, Germany
Pnina Soffer	University of Haifa, Israel
Sandra Zilker	Technische Hochschule Nürnberg Georg Simon Ohm, Germany

Additional Reviewers

Michalis Mountantonakis

Contents

CMLS

AviFluHunt: Model, Database, and Tool for Flexible Querying of Avian Influenza Genomes

Anna Bernasconi(✉), Tommaso Alfonsi, Luca Cassenti, and Pietro Pinoli

Dipartimento di Elettronica, Informazione e Bioingegneria, Politecnico di Milano, Milan, Italy
anna.bernasconi@polimi.it

Abstract. Influenza has shaped human history for millennia, with avian influenza recently posing challenges due to its potential for cross-species transmission and the risk of triggering pandemics that could hurt both human populations and livestock industries. Avian influenza, the focus of this work, is known to primarily affect birds, both domestic and wild, causing outbreaks worldwide. Furthermore, reports of cross-species transmission of avian flu viruses from livestock to humans are becoming increasingly common, which, while not an immediate issue, could become problematic were one of these viruses to become dangerous to humans. This work introduces AviFluHunt, a tool specifically developed to help with the analysis of bulk data on avian influenza samples, to enable more effective genomic surveillance and timely responses to the virus's evolution. A set of queries of interest was created to help answer questions of significance for virologists. We focus on tracking genetic markers, understanding viral mutations, and examining essential metadata, including host species, geographical regions, and temporal trends. AviFluHunt processes large datasets of genomic sequences with metadata through a bioinformatic pipeline and presents results in a custom web application, designed to make them accessible and interpretable for researchers.

AviFluHunt stands as a lightweight Web application that provides accurate data insights and identifies trends/interesting behaviors associated with avian flu viruses, offering researchers and virologists a new asset for their studies, thereby enhancing their understanding of the virus.

Keywords: Viral Sequences · Genomic Data Modeling · Avian Influenza

1 Introduction

Wild waterfowl, particularly migratory birds, are natural reservoir of avian influenza and play an important role in spreading the virus across large geographical areas. Infected birds can contaminate environments, increasing the risk

P. Fettke et al. (Eds.): ER 2026, LNCS 17125, pp. 3–19, 2027.
https://doi.org/10.1007/978-3-032-40377-3_1

to domestic animals and, occasionally, to humans [38]. Among avian influenza viruses, the highly pathogenic H5N1 subtype has become a major concern for genomic surveillance [29]. In particular, viruses belonging to the clade 2.3.4.4b [21] have spread globally and recently demonstrated an unprecedented host range, including the 2024–2025 spillover into dairy cattle in the United States [31].

These developments have reinforced the importance of genomic surveillance. International organizations, including the World Health Organization and the European Food Safety Authority [20,38], have identified continuous genome sequencing and data sharing as fundamental components of preparedness against emerging influenza threats. Concurrently, the GISAID EpiFlu database [34] has grown to include more than 50,000 H5N1 isolates (i.e., viral samples), corresponding to over 350,000 segment sequences (July 2026), with continuous data depositions. Numerous genetic markers have been associated with phenotypes (e.g., mammalian adaptation, antiviral resistance, altered receptor binding, and increased virulence [35]). Monitoring these mutations across rapidly growing genomic datasets is essential for identifying emerging variants that may pose increased risks to animal or human health [31], together with other evolutionary mechanisms such as intra-segment recombination [4,6] or reassortment [2,5].

While repositories such as GISAID provide access to influenza genome sequences, extracting biologically meaningful subsets of genomes often requires complex combinations of metadata, genomic markers, and temporal or geographical constraints. Existing resources provide limited support for flexible querying across these heterogeneous dimensions, making large-scale exploratory analyses cumbersome. To address these challenges, we present AviFluHunt, a flexible platform for systematically querying H5N1 influenza data across sequence, mutation, host, spatial, and temporal dimensions. Our contributions include:

- A *conceptual data model* and *relational database schema* capturing influenza genomes, genomic segments, molecular markers, associated phenotypic effects, and epidemiological metadata.
- A *reproducible bioinformatics pipeline* for automatically populating the database from publicly available (or private) genomic datasets.
- A set of *relevant domain-expert-designed queries*, extracting insights within the data, allowing filters by location, date range, or (taxonomy-grounded) host types.
- An *interactive web dashboard* to explore the results provided by the queries, distributed as a *Docker application* to facilitate deployment on both public and private datasets.

In the following, Sect. 2 recapitulates related works. Section 3 provides an overview of the database schema used to store data. Section 4 describes methods, including a bioinformatic pipeline that extracts, transforms, and loads the data into the AviFluHunt database. Section 5 describes the Web application, including software architecture, front-end interface, query modules, and Docker container distributed openly. Section 6 proposes three relevant use cases to appreciate the immediate interaction offered by the AviFluHunt tool. Finally, Sect. 7 enumerates the benefits and limitations of our proposal.

2 Related Work

Search systems and databases dedicated to influenza genomics provide essential platforms for gathering, analyzing, and sharing virus-related genetic information on a global scale. The first major platform is provided by GISAID [34], a global project launched in 2008 to provide access to influenza genomic data. NCBI Virus [14] is a viral database provided by the National Library of Medicine (NIH), with more than 1.7M protein sequences on influenza viruses, of which around 1.5M are of Type A. The Influenza Research Database (IRD) [25], funded by the US NIH/NIAID, is a bioinformatics platform that supports the search, analysis, and visualization of influenza virus data. The Bacterial and Viral Bioinformatics Resource Center (BV-BRC) [36] is an information system that supports research on bacterial and viral infectious diseases.

Modern research platforms for Influenza and other pathogens also offer advanced analytical tools. FluSurver [28] aids the research community in the identification, analysis, and interpretation of mutations within influenza sequences. INSaFLU [32] is a free, web-based bioinformatics suite designed to analyze primary sequencing data. FluMut [22] is an open-source tool specifically designed to identify molecular markers that may impact the biological characteristics of influenza A viruses, particularly the H5N1 subtype.

During the surge of SARS-CoV-2, we proposed models for storing coronaviruses sequences metadata [9,13,16], epitopes [11], and corresponding clinical [10] or literature-derived [3] knowledge; this work was inspired by previous efforts to model human genome data [12,18]. Here, we aim to transfer these high-level modeling principles to the case of avian influenza viruses, where the main difference stands in the more complex structure.

3 Database Schema

The database model is shown in Fig. 1, using a classical relational logical schema notation [8]. The schema presents three thematic dimensions:

(1) The *SequenceData dimension* (pink, top of Fig. 1) is concerned with representing SEGMENTs and their MUTATIONs (with respect to a REFERENCE-SEGMENT) – connected through the bridge table SEGMENTMUTATION. The actual continuous string of a genome segment is stored in SEGMENTDATA; it is then connected to multiple ANNOTATIONs (i.e., proteins) that potentially include non-continuous fragments (called INTEINs).
(2) The *Metadata dimension* (green, bottom left of Fig. 1) represents auxiliary information of a segment; this pertains to a single ISOLATE, which presents a specific collection LOCATION and derives from a certain HOST organism (storing unique host_id and the scientific name); the host may have a related

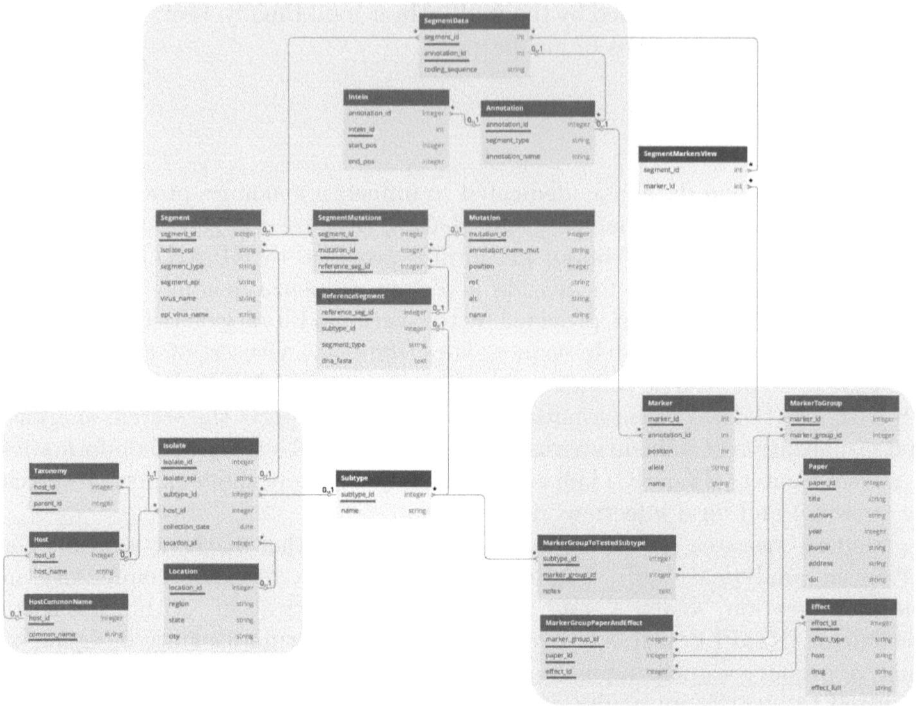

Fig. 1. AviFluHunt database logical schema for data storing and querying.

HostCommonName (possibly sharred by different hosts) – we maintain a denormalized structure of hosts in the Taxonomy table, which stores parent-child relationships to rebuild the taxonomic hierarchy.

(3) The *Marker dimension* (blue, bottom right of Fig. 1) describes single Markers. These are connected to the *SequenceData dimension* through Annotations (each Marker is located on one Annotation, while one Annotation may contain multiple Markers). Additionally, a materialized view (SegmentMarkersView) connects two tables across the dimensions. Markers can be grouped (according to the mapping expressed in MarkerToGroup). Each group has been tested on subtypes (MarkerGroupToTestedSubtype) and connected to some Paper with reported Effect, through the triple bridge table MarkerGroupPaperAndEffect.

Note that the Subtype information connects all three dimensions, being relevant to characterize Isolates, ReferenceSegments, and MarkerGroups. It allows extending the model from H5N1 (subtype instance) to all Influenza A viruses.

The schema is composed of tables and relationships. All tables have a list of attributes; those forming the primary key (PK) are underlined, and attribute types are reported. PKs are a numerical sequence conventionally named using the table name and the postfix "_id" (or formed by multiple fields). Relationships are defined among pairs of tables, drawn as links connecting pairs of attributes; we indicate with foreign keys the relationships from a non-key attribute to a primary key attribute of a different table. Cardinalities are expressed on both sides of the relationship; they are indicated according to the classical notation in ER diagrams [8]: one Isolate contains possibly multiple (*) Segments, whereas one Segment pertains to none or one (0..1) Isolate; many-to-many relationships (with * on both sides) connect, for instance, MarkerToGroup to the respective MarkerGroupToTestedSubtype and MarkerGroupPaperAndEffect, and viceversa.

4 Methods

Our methods are source-agnostic, as they can be applied to any dataset that follows our format and semantics requisites. Ideally, our tool can be employed with freshly downloaded data from GISAID, from any user who can access Influenza data through authentication.

The data manager runs a bioinformatic pipeline processing the dataset and the related metadata; it creates the database, which is filled with the sequence data. We employ Python scripts to create the DB schema from a `.sql` file; we use the SQLite database engine, easily embeddable in Web applications.

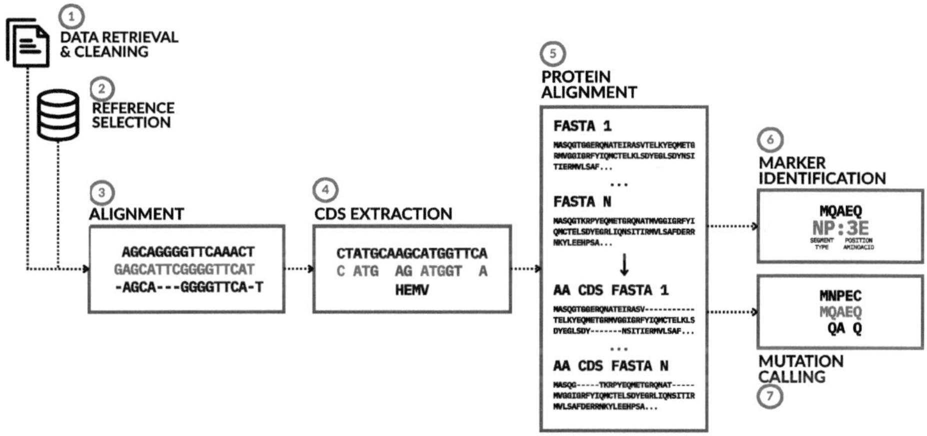

Fig. 2. Bioinformatic pipeline steps.

4.1 Data Processing Pipeline

Genomic data from influenza isolates is processed through a specialized data pipeline (Fig. 2) with the following steps:

(1) **Data retrieval and cleaning.** The framework expects its input in the multi-FASTA format, i.e., a collection of one or more sequences, each composed of one line containing the nucleotide sequence, with the specific header "DNA Accession no. | Segment | Virus name | Isolate ID | Type". A metadata file (in the .xls format) is expected to contain one line per sequence – we follow the typical format of GISAID, where each line has: i) Isolate ID (associates each row to a specific isolate); ii) eight columns, one for each segment, containing the IDs of the (up to) eight segment sequences—'NA' is employed to indicate when one is not available; iii) Isolate Name (a verbose human-readable name); iv) Location, where the biological sample was collected; v) Host, the kind of organism from which the sample was sourced; and vi) Date, indicating the date of collection. After data downloading (or in-house preparation), sequence data are filtered to ensure quality. Sequences containing erroneous nucleotides (i.e., bases different from A, T, C, G) are excluded. Sequences with excessive missing data (typically represented by gaps or the "–" symbol) are removed. Sequences exceeding the maximum threshold of 5% are also discarded.

(2) **Reference segments.** We require reference sequences for all 8 segments (sourced from FluMut [22] or the NCBI database [14]). For the subtype H5N1, we employ the widely-accepted `A/Goose/Guangdong/1/96` reference sequence.

(3) **Alignment.** We align each isolate's segment to the related reference sequence at the nucleotide level. We employed the AUGUR tool [24] using the MAFFT aligner [30], which, given a file containing a reference and one with one or more FASTA sequences, outputs i) a file with the aligned sequences and ii) a file with insertions.

(4) **CDS extraction.** We extract the coding sequence regions (CDS) of each segment, i.e., the portion of the genome responsible for coding the protein. Inputs are the aligned sequences and the extra file with all the insertions necessary to complete each segment (output in step 3); these are indicated using coordinates that refer to the chosen reference sequence. Each segment is considered together with the information on the coding sequences for the specific segment type of the segment (e.g., each MP segment codifies two proteins, called M1 and M2, using different parts of the genome whose positions are standard). If any insertion is indicated, we check if it falls inside the boundaries of the coding file. In this case, its nucleotides are added to the genetic sequence; otherwise, they are discarded. During this process, we keep track of how many nucleotides are added (to update the length of the coding sequences). After all the insertions have been added to the RNA sequences, the coding sequences are extracted (one for each protein codified by the segment of the isolate), taking into account the insertions. The coding sequences are then cleaned by removing deletions (represented as a '-' in the sequences). Finally, the RNA sequences that are aligned, cleaned, and translated into amino acid sequences.

(5) **(5) Protein alignment.** We perform a second-level alignment that uses the amino acid sequences, specifically to realign the sequences to the reference

segments, as adding insertions and removing deletions before translating the RNA sequence can affect the relative positioning. The process is conceptually similar to the RNA alignment and uses the same tools described above.

(6) **(6) Markers.** Scientific literature was derived from various sources, all described by [35], structured in a machine-readable format in [22]: a collection of all the scientific data on Markers to date, divided by segment, using the position numbering suggested by Burke et al. [15] for HA segments. For identifying markers, we employ the SegmentMarkersView, used to compare the marker's amino acid residue with the one in the sequence at the marker's position (relative to the corresponding coding sequence).

(7) **Mutations.** For mutations, we employ an internally-developed pipeline for Variant Calling (10.5281/zenodo.14181633), designed to detect mutations given a sequence, a reference, and the insertion file provided by the AUGUR alignment tool. The output is then saved by the program in the database. The used tool makes it possible to extract mutations from a reference file and a file comprising one or more FASTA sequences aligned with the selected reference. The output of the tool, also in Python, is a dictionary that associates each sequence ID in the FASTA file with three lists of mutations: i) amino acid level substitutions (expressed as REF_AA:POSITION:ALT_AA); ii) insertions (_:POSITION:ALT_AA); and iii) deletions (REF_AA:POSITION:_).

Example Database Instance. To demonstrate AviFluHunt, we downloaded data on February 17th, 2025; in this example instance, we only consider the H5N1 subtype, but the database is designed to accommodate many different ones at the same time. In the following, when referring to the data amount, we refer to this example dataset. We retrieved a total of 31,715 unique H5N1 virus isolates, including 193,431 different segments (of 8 types). Each segment can encode for one to three proteins (we consider 17 "inteins"). More than 28K protein-level locations were identified as potential mutations (i.e., mutated in at least one instance of the database). Isolates are derived from a plethora of different geographic locations (~1,300) and 291 hosts. For the absolute majority of them (289), we were able to link a specific taxonomic ID from the NCBI Taxonomy [33] so that synonyms/hypernyms/hyponyms can be retrieved easily. We considered 254 markers, which are represented in 473 groups, each connected to one of 101 different effects; effects are supported by a bibliography of 404 scientific papers and tested on different subtypes (56, not all necessarily H5N1).

4.2 Host Inference and Taxonomy-Driven Search

The taxonomy-handling module was developed to ensure a consistent, structured, and automated way of assigning host information to each isolate inserted into the database. Host names are often provided in free text within metadata, either as scientific names, common names, or even slightly incorrect or incomplete forms. To tackle this, we implemented a taxonomy enrichment system that leverages both local data and external services.

For each isolate record in the original dataset, we retrieve the information and automatically match it to an entry in the NCBI Taxonomy [33] (sourced from the NCBI Entrez API), containing both their official scientific names and various alternative or common names, extracted based on the name type field (e.g., "scientific name", "common name", "synonym"). This enriched local taxonomy is used to support fuzzy matching and rapid lookups.

When a new isolate is retrieved, with its host metadata string, we try three strategies in order: 1) Direct match (i.e., containment in the HostCommonName table, being a valid scientific name). 2) Manual input (i.e., containment in a domain-expert manually curated dictionary, loaded from manual_tax.xlsx). 3) Fuzzy matching (i.e., we use the `rapidfuzz` library [7], trying to find a likely match among all known scientific and common names; here we employ a filtering process to ensure the matched species is within a desired family, e.g., Aves or Mammalia, using the `taxoniq` Python library [26]).

If a match is found, a new record is created in the Host and HostCommonName tables, and linked to the isolate through the `host_id` attribute – the entire taxonomical hierarchy is built (from the host up until the 'Aves' root) and stored in the Taxonomy table. Else, the host is left as null (this occurs in a minority of cases, for 850 isolates out of 31.7k).

5 Web Application

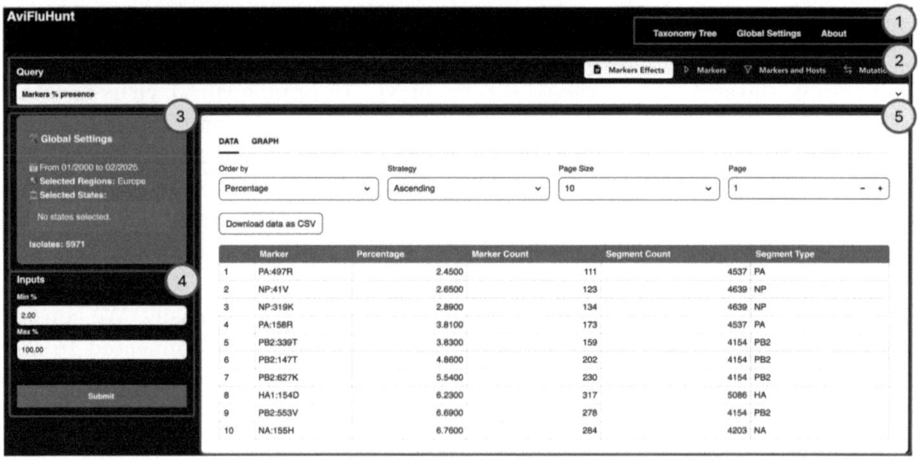

Fig. 3. Web Interface sections: (1) Navigation Bar; (2) Query Selector ('Markers % presence' has been selected); (3) Global Settings Summary; (4) Parameter Setter; (5) Results Panel.

AviFluHunt is implemented as a web application, accessible through a web browser (see Fig. 3); it has an interactive and user-friendly interface with five sections:

(1) The *Navigation Bar* allows access to the avian taxonomy explorer tool (working as described in the "Methods"); the selector of global settings (location filters on Continent and Country and a Collection Date interval); and a page with acknowledgements.
(2) The *Query Selector* allows the selection of one of four macro groups of queries (on the right), including those on markers' effects, markers' analysis, the relationship between markers and hosts, and mutations; on the left, a dynamically populated drop-down menu exposes the list of queries within each group. The full list of queries is provided in Table 1.
(3) The *Global Settings Summary* recapitulates dataset filters; global filters affect all run queries (except those not concerning isolates/sequence counts).
(4) The *Parameter Selector* accommodates optional parameters that define the scope of the executed query (incorporated in the query at submission). Options include, e.g., marker name, effect type, host type, or numerical filters.
(5) The *Results Panel* shows query outputs in a table or graph form, equipped with an option to download the data or the graph.

5.1 Implementation

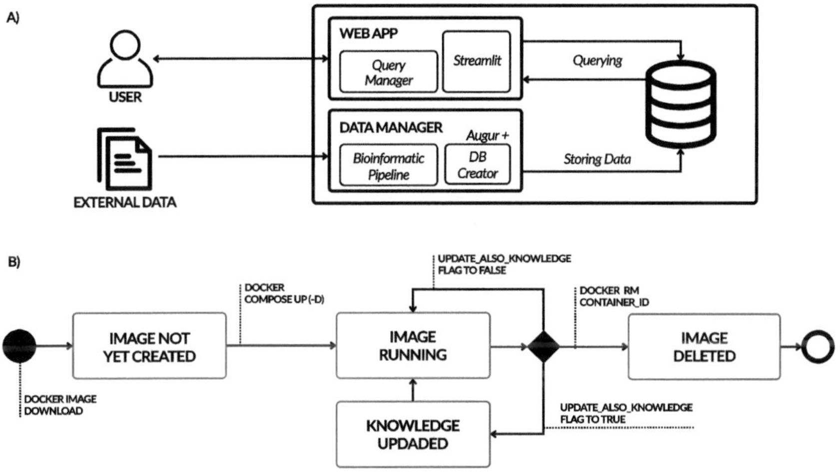

Fig. 4. Panel A) describes the tool's architecture. Panel B) describes the Docker container state diagram.

The system architecture is shown in Fig. 4A. External data is input in the Data Manager, including a Bioinformatic pipeline and a Database creator. Data is persisted in a SQLite database. The database is queried from the application

Table 1. List of queries available on AviFluHunt, divided into four sections, each focused on a different aspect and dimension of the Database schema in Fig. 1.

Markers Effect	Literature references per group of markers	Inputs: List of marker names Output: Table of relevant literature entries (DOI, publication, etc.) discussing the specific group of markers
	Marker groups with specific marker	Inputs: Marker name. Output: Table listing associated marker groups and their descriptions
	Effects associated with specific host or drug	Inputs: Host name (e.g., human, chicken) or drug name Output: Table of markers, known effect descriptions (e.g., transmissibility, drug resistance) possibly tied to specific host/drug
	Marker groups associated with specific effect	Inputs: Effect description Output: Table of marker groups linked to the specified effect (e.g., âĂIJincreased transmission in humansâĂİ)
Markers	Markers % presence	Inputs: Min-max percentage range of interest. Output: Table or chart showing marker frequency counts/percentages over the relevant segments
	Markers % presence per specific segment/host	Inputs: Segment type and host type. Output: Table of markers in specified segment, count of isolates from specified host, with associated groups
	Location distribution per specific marker	Inputs: Marker name. Output: Table or chart showing how often the specified marker appears in each location (country, region, etc.), normalized by the total isolates in that location
	Prevalence in time per specific marker	Input: List of marker names. Output: Table or chart showing time series of markers' prevalence (in segments)
Markers and Hosts	Host distribution per specific marker	Inputs: Marker name. Output: Table or chart of host distribution over isolates
	Markers by relative % of human isolates	Inputs: Segment type, percentage range, and minimum n. of isolates. Output: Table of markers with their relative frequency in humans (w.r.t. other hosts)
	Markers by difference in hosts' presence	Inputs: Two or more host types for comparison. Output: Table showing marker name, percentage in two (or more) host types, difference in percentage between the first two host types
	Markers' comparison in hosts' presence	Inputs: One or more host types for comparison. Output: Table showing marker name, percentage in one (or more) host types
	Distribution of distinct markers per host type	Inputs: Segment type. Output: Table or chart showing counts of isolates with any marker per host type
Mutations	Mutations on genomic regions	Inputs: Annotation type (within segments); i) user-defined coordinate intervals or ii) fixed region size and offset. Output: Table or chart indicating, for each region, the number of distinct mutations and the Mut. isol. ratio
	Temporal distribution of mutations	Inputs: Segment type and minimum n. of segments. Output: Table or chart indicating the mutation/segment ratio per single month – drawing a time series

and provides results to be visualised. Users interact with the Web Application, including the Query Manager and the Streamlit app manager.

The tool has been packaged into a Docker installation [17], making it usable by any user or lab practitioner who wishes to run it on a prepared set of data documents. The only requirements on format are those described in the "Methods" (Data processing pipeline section). In our system, we distinguish: 1) *static knowledge*, including reference segments, information on markers, subtypes, inteins, annotations, papers, and effects; 2) *dynamic data*, i.e., the actual viral genome sequences.

Setting up the running Docker involves: a `docker-compose.yml` file for configuration; an `.env` (environment) file (containing location paths of data and metadata, and a boolean flag for enabling static knowledge updates); and folders for static knowledge and dynamic data content. The Docker image, shared on our code repository [17], comes with selected pre-packaged data, such as the reference segments for the H5N1 subtype. Other data types are configured by the user according to needs.

The detailed state diagram of the system is described in Fig. 4B). First, the Docker image needs to be downloaded. After files' configuration and setting `update_also_knowledge = TRUE` in the environment file, the Docker can be started. Three possible modes are available: 1) Running the image without updating the database; 2) Running the image updating only dynamic data (`update_also_knowledge = FALSE`); 3) Running the image, updating also static knowledge (`update_also_knowledge = TRUE`).

6 Use Cases

Exploiting the global settings selector, we select isolates from North America from January 2020 to February 2025 (until the 17th, as included in our example DB instance), for a total of 13,400 isolates. Next, we demonstrate the AviFluHunt application with an exploratory analysis of this dataset, exploiting four different queries.

Marker Groups, their Effects, and Temporal Prevalence. With the 'Marker groups with specific marker' query within the MARKERS EFFECT group, we select the HA1:103Y (meaning that the Tyrosine amino acid residue is present on the 103 position of the HA1 subunit of the HA segment). In Fig. 5A, we appreciate the list of markers' groups that include the selected one, each associated with the specific effect, i.e., "Airborne transmissible in ferrets" according to reference literature [23,27,35].

By combining this analysis with the 'Location distribution per specific marker' query in the MARKERS group and removing the global filters previously set, we can observe that this marker is particularly present in Ukraine (>4% normalized presence, which is significantly higher than other locations around the world).

While HA1:103Y is quite rare in the North American population, other markers in the listed groups have been more widely represented in this geographical area. By leveraging the 'Prevalence in time per specific marker' query within the MARKERS group, we can extract counts (and percentages) of segments exhibiting a specific marker by year. As can be observed in Fig. 5B, among the markers presented in Panel A, HA1:156A is by far the most present one through 2022–2024 (within thousands of isolates); PB2:627K was also found in about 20 isolates per year.

A combination of different queries found in the MARKERS and MARKERS EFFECT groups allows a broad analysis of markers studied for H5N1 in user-selected populations of genomic sequences, with wide freedom in the choice of filters on location, prevalence in time, segment, tested host or drug.

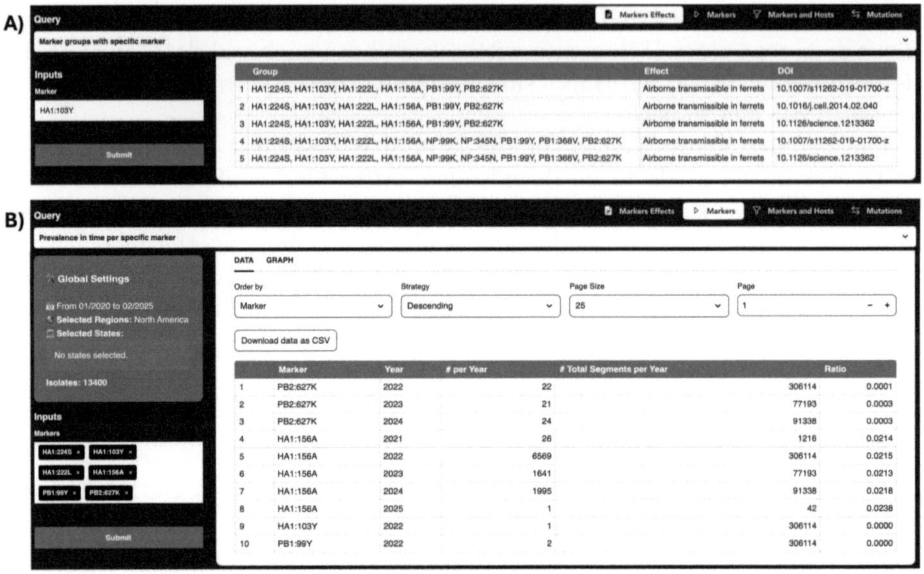

Fig. 5. Investigating effect groups including HA1:103Y. Panel A) describes the output of the query 'Marker groups with specific marker' when HA1:103Y is selected. Panel B) describes the output of 'Prevalence in time per specific marker' when a group of markers, taken from panel A), is considered.

Markers' Preference in Hosts. With the 'Markers by difference in hosts' presence' query within the MARKERS AND HOSTS group, we can investigate an interesting phenomenon: how different host groups are infected by isolates that show differences in specific markers (in percentage). This query largely leverages the host taxonomy mappings. In Fig. 6A, we select three partitions of avians, namely the Galliformes order (ground-feeding birds), the Anseriformes group (ducks, geese & swans), and the Passeriformes order (song birds). Interestingly, when we sort markers by their relative presence in Galliformes and Anseriformes, we obtain that two markers on PB1 (PB1-F2:56A and PB1:207R) have a 3.5–5% higher prevalence in Galliformes, suggesting that viruses with these markers may be more fit to these kinds of birds. A similar happening could also be further investigated for PA markers, namely PA:497R and PA:400P. The methodological work to link host-related metadata to a taxonomical structure is fundamental to allow users seamless selection of orders/groups and distinguish different levels of depth in the hierarchy. Our taxonomy allows us to select any kind of host present in the NCBI taxonomy within Aves (or some -limited choice- among mammals).

Considering much more distant organisms, Fig. 5B offers a comparison including Aves, Bos taurus (Dairy Cow), and Homo Sapiens (Human); here, the position 66S on PB1-F2 protein was prioritized as more present in avian rather than mammals and humans. This finding is particularly interesting as it confirms previously acquired knowledge on the single N66S amino acid change that correlates with pathogenicity and increased virulence, characterized during the 1997 Hong Kong H5N1 outbreak [19,37].

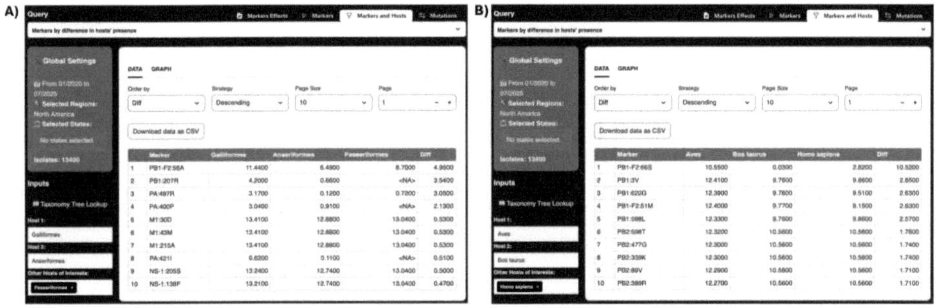

Fig. 6. Markers ordered by difference in their presence across different hosts. Panel A) describes the output of the query 'Markers by difference in hosts' presence' when three host names are selected (Galliformes, Anseriformes, Passeriformes). Panel B) describes the output of the same query when the other three host names (much larger) are selected (Aves, Bos Taurus, Homo Sapiens).

Stable Regions. With the 'Mutations on genomic regions' query within the MUTATIONS group, we can investigate the rate of mutation in certain areas of the virus and how it evolves through time. On Zhu et al. [40], we gathered that HA1 has polar residues from fragments 53 to 62, 78 to 83, 117 to 119, and 273 to 278 in the vestigial esterase domain, which are known to be quite stable areas - previously used for epitopes [40]. In Table 2, we summarize the search we operated on AviFluHunt by exploiting the 'manual regions' insertion option. We employed the four intervals indicated in [40] and consequently repeated the query for four different time intervals, namely the long stretch 2010–2021 (for which only 60 isolates were present in North America), then the years 2022, 2023, and 2024.

For each time interval and genome segment (genome range on the HA segment), we collect i) the absolute number of distinct mutations occurring in the specified range and ii) the ratio of mutations on each segment (i.e., 1 means that each segment exhibits, on average, one mutation). While clearly the time intervals have very different numerosity, and the first period (2010–2021) has quite uneven observations, in the following three intervals (2022–2024), some trend can be observed, with all HA ranges slightly increasing the ratio of mutations per segment over time – as indicated in Table 2. E.g., the 253–278 range went from harboring about 1.001 mutations (in 2022), to 1.0025 mutations (in 2023), to almost 1.003 (in 2024), with the highest increase being of 53–62 mutations in 2024. Extracting the overlap of epitopes with sequences is a very relevant task. The rationale is to allow intersection between interval-based data triggering immune response (epitopes) and interval-based data representing the viral evolution (genome sequences with mutations and markers). This computation allows to prioritize areas that are typically hit by a higher mutation rate; these need to be checked, as the efficacy of any drugs or treatment previously based on them could be compromised. This principle was previously adopted on SARS-CoV-2 data [1,11].

Table 2. Number of distinct types of mutations and mutations' ratio per segment in the specified HA coordinates ranges in four periods (2010–2021, years 2022, 2023, 2024).

HA range	Length	Jan 2010–Dec 2021 (60 is.)		Jan–Dec 2022 (6754 is.)		Jan–Dec 2023 (1664 is.)		Jan–Dec 2024 (2239 is.)	
		#Dist. mut.	#Mut./segm.	#Dist. mut.	#Mut./segm.	#Dist. mut.	#Mut./segm.	#Dist. mut.	#Mut./segm.
53–62	6	6	1	7	0.0011	3	0.0018	6	0.1144
78–83	3	1	0.0169	3	0.0008	1	0.0018	1	0.0054
117–119	26	1	0.0169	2	0.0005	0	0	3	0.0029
253–278	1	9	1.0508	11	1.0091	10	1.0255	32	1.0295

7 Conclusion

The emergence and rapid spread of highly pathogenic avian influenza H5N1 highlighted the urgent need for tools that enable timely and flexible exploration of viral sequence data. AviFluHunt addresses this gap as –with a lightweight installation procedure– it allows researchers, public health authorities, and policymakers to query and interpret H5N1 sequence datasets equipped with literature information from markers and effects. Overall, this tool can facilitate the detection of emerging mutations, host-specific adaptations, and geographic dissemination patterns.

In our three use cases, we showcased examples of use where the tool allowed us to identify trends of markers in space and in time, study the different distribution of markers in hosts, and observe the stability of epitope-selected regions of the genome. These encompass a series of possible applications of the proposed web service, which is designed to be as easy to use as possible and also responsive for answering user-generated hypotheses, with a reactive interface. The time required by data analysis is short and does not depend on either the size of the initial dataset or the specific kind of analysis, as data aggregations are computed at loading time. AviFluHunt can be extended in the future by adding more 'query panels' as needed by groups of users – the modular design of both its database and user interface makes it easy to implement further functionalities to answer specific research questions.

By lowering the technical barriers to exploratory analyses, AviFluHunt empowers a broader range of users to generate hypotheses and respond to evolving threats, complementing established surveillance systems and analytical pipelines. More generally, AviFluHunt's effort aligns to the broader vision of FAIR data-based genomic surveillance by facilitating the organization, exploration, and reuse of genomic sequences and their associated metadata [39]. In the H5N1 epidemic context, such capability can guide risk assessments and inform the prioritization of interventions.

While the use and impact of AviFluHunt is limited to H5N1 avian influenza (along with the choices made in FluMut [22]), it remains possible to extend this work to include all other subtypes, opening much larger possibilities of analysis, especially for other H5-based subtypes. However, we note that this process is not straightforward for other subtypes and requires further research on how to adapt marker positions across subtypes (see [15,35]). The current installation procedure through Docker requires some technical expertise; however, we adopted this solution as it allows every user to employ the tool on their own dataset, without the need for data sharing.

Overall, AviFluHunt's simple paradigm could be reapplied to any kind of dataset with similar characteristics, also in the context of possible future pandemics.

Acknowledgement. This research was supported by the project BETTER (Grant agreement n. 101136262).

References

1. Al Khalaf, R., et al.: Systematic analysis of SARS-CoV-2 Omicron subvariants' impact on B and T cell epitopes. PLoS ONE **19**(9), e0307873 (2024)
2. Alfonsi, T., Bernasconi, A., Chiara, M., Ceri, S.: Lightweight multiscale early warning system for influenza a spillovers. Sci. Adv. **11**(43), eadz7312 (2025)
3. Alfonsi, T., et al.: CoV2K model, a comprehensive representation of SARS-CoV-2 knowledge and data interplay. Sci. Data **9**(1), 260 (2022)
4. Alfonsi, T., et al.: Data-driven recombination detection in viral genomes. Nat. Commun. **15**(1), 3313 (2024)
5. Alfonsi, T., et al.: A codon usage-based approach for the stratification of Influenza A across recent spillovers. Comput. Struct. Biotechnol. J. **27**, 2757–2771 (2025)
6. Alfonsi, T., et al.: OpenRecombinHunt: automatic detection of recombination in publicly available viral sequences. J. Molec. Biol. 169811 (2026)
7. Bachmann, M.: Rapid fuzzy string matching in Python and C++ using the Levenshtein Distance. pypi.org/project/RapidFuzz/. Accessed 6 July 2026
8. Batini, C., et al.: Conceptual Database Design: An Entity-Relationship Approach. Benjamin-Cummings series in computer science, Redwood City, CA (1992)
9. Bernasconi, A., Canakoglu, A., Pinoli, P., Ceri, S.: Empowering virus sequence research through conceptual modeling. In: Dobbie, G., Frank, U., Kappel, G., Liddle, S.W., Mayr, H.C. (eds.) ER 2020. LNCS, vol. 12400, pp. 388–402. Springer, Cham (2020). https://doi.org/10.1007/978-3-030-62522-1_29
10. Bernasconi, A., et al.: A review on viral data sources and search systems for perspective mitigation of COVID-19. Brief. Bioinf. **22**(2), 664–675 (2021)
11. Bernasconi, A., et al.: EpiSurf: metadata-driven search server for analyzing amino acid changes within epitopes of SARS-CoV-2 and other viral species. Database **2021**, baab059 (2021)

12. Bernasconi, A.: A comprehensive approach for the conceptual modeling of genomic data. In: International Conference on Conceptual Modeling, pp. 194–208. Springer, Heidelberg (2022). https://doi.org/10.1007/978-3-031-17995-2_14
13. Bernasconi, A., et al.: Semantic interoperability: ontological unpacking of a viral conceptual model. BMC Bioinf. **23**(Suppl 11), 491 (2022)
14. Brister, J.R., et al.: NCBI viral genomes resource. Nucleic Acids Res. **43**(D1), D571–D577 (2015)
15. Burke, D.F., Smith, D.J.: A recommended numbering scheme for influenza A HA subtypes. PLoS ONE **9**(11), e112302 (2014)
16. Canakoglu, A., et al.: ViruSurf: an integrated database to investigate viral sequences. Nucleic Acids Res. **49**(D1), D817–D824 (2021)
17. Cassenti, L., et al.: AviFluHunt GitHub Code Repository, github.com/DEIB-GECO/AviFluHunt-repo/. Accessed 6 July 2026
18. Ceri, S., et al.: Overview of GeCo: a project for exploring and integrating signals from the genome. In: Kalinichenko, L., Manolopoulos, Y., Malkov, O., Skvortsov, N., Stupnikov, S., Sukhomlin, V. (eds.) DAMDID/RCDL 2017. CCIS, vol. 822, pp. 46–57. Springer, Cham (2018). https://doi.org/10.1007/978-3-319-96553-6_4
19. Conenello, G.M., et al.: A single mutation in the PB1-F2 of H5N1 (HK/97) and 1918 influenza A viruses contributes to increased virulence. PLoS Pathog. **3**(10), e141 (2007)
20. EFSA: Avian influenza | efsa. efsa.europa.eu/en/topics/topic/avian-influenza. Accessed 6 July 2026
21. Fusaro, A., et al.: High pathogenic avian influenza A (H5) viruses of clade 2.3.4.4b in Europe—why trends of virus evolution are more difficult to predict. Virus Evol. **10**(1), veae027 (2024)
22. Giussani, E., et al.: FluMut: a tool for mutation surveillance in highly pathogenic H5N1 genomes. Virus Evol. **11**(1), veaf011 (2025)
23. Herfst, S.: Airborne transmission of influenza A/H5N1 virus between ferrets. Science **336**(6088), 1534–1541 (2012)
24. Huddleston, J.: Augur: a bioinformatics toolkit for phylogenetic analyses of human pathogens. J. Open Source Software **6**(57) (2021)
25. JCV Institute: Influenza research database (2017). jcvi.org/research/influenza-research-database-ird. Accessed 6 July 2026
26. Kislyuk, A.: Taxoniq: Taxon Information Query - fast, offline querying of NCBI Taxonomy and related data. pypi.org/project/taxoniq/. Accessed 6 July 2026
27. Linster, M., et al.: Identification, characterization, and natural selection of mutations driving airborne transmission of A/H5N1 virus. Cell **157**(2), 329–339 (2014)
28. Maurer Stroh, S., et al.: FluSurver - Influenza Surveillance - Prepared for the next wave (2009). flusurver.bii.a-star.edu.sg. Accessed 6 July 2026
29. Morens, D.M., et al.: Many potential pathways to future pandemic influenza. Sci. Transl. Med. **15**(718), eadj2379 (2023)
30. Nakamura, T., et al.: Parallelization of MAFFT for large-scale multiple sequence alignments. Bioinformatics **34**(14), 2490–2492 (2018)
31. Nguyen, T.Q., et al.: Emergence and interstate spread of highly pathogenic avian influenza A (H5N1) in dairy cattle in the United States. Science **388**(6745), eadq0900 (2025)
32. Santos, J.D., et al.: INSaFLU-TELEVIR: an open web-based bioinformatics suite for viral metagenomic detection and routine genomic surveillance. Genome Med. **16**(1), 61 (2024)
33. Schoch, C.L., et al.: NCBI taxonomy: a comprehensive update on curation, resources and tools. Database **2020**, baaa062 (2020)

34. Shu, Y., McCauley, J.: GISAID: Global initiative on sharing all influenza data–from vision to reality. Eurosurveillance **22**(13) (2017)
35. Suttie, A., Deng, Y.-M., Greenhill, A.R., Dussart, P., Horwood, P.F., Karlsson, E.A.: Inventory of molecular markers affecting biological characteristics of avian influenza A viruses. Virus Genes **55**(6), 739–768 (2019). https://doi.org/10.1007/s11262-019-01700-z
36. University of Chicago: Bacterial and viral bioinformatics resource center (2024). bv-brc.org/. Accessed 6 July 2026
37. Varga, Z.T., et al.: The influenza virus protein PB1-F2 inhibits the induction of type I interferon at the level of the MAVS adaptor protein. PLoS Pathog. **7**(6), e1002067 (2011)
38. WHOA: Avian Influenza - WHOA - World Organization for Animal Health. woah.org/en/disease/avian-influenza/
39. Wilkinson, M.D., et al.: The FAIR Guiding Principles for scientific data management and stewardship. Sci. Data **3**, 160018 (2016)
40. Zhu, X., et al.: A unique and conserved neutralization epitope in H5N1 influenza viruses identified by an antibody against the A/Goose/Guangdong/1/96 hemagglutinin. J. Virol. **87**(23), 12619–12635 (2013)

Conceptual Modeling for Semantically-Guided Feature Selection in Machine Learning: A Case Study on Mohs Micrographic Surgery

Francisco Miralles Ferrer[1(✉)], Edu Nagore Insa[1(✉)], Salvador Francisco Navarro Aljibe[1], Ruggero Moro[2,3], Eduardo Nagore Enguídanos[3], and Oscar Pastor[1]

[1] Valencian Research Institute for Artificial Intelligence (VRAIN), Universitat Politècnica de València, Valencia, Spain
{fmirfer,enagins}@vrain.upv.es
[2] Escuela de Doctorado, Universidad Católica de Valencia San Vicente Martir, Valencia, Spain
[3] Servicio de Dermatología, Instituto Valenciano de Oncología, Valencia, Spain

Abstract. The increasing adoption of Machine Learning in healthcare has highlighted the challenges of conducting experiments on biomedical datasets characterized by limited sample sizes and numerous clinical variables. Traditional feature selection techniques are mainly based on statistical or optimization criteria and may overlook the semantic relationships that exist between clinical variables.

This paper proposes the use of Conceptual Modeling as a semantic framework to support feature grouping in Machine Learning experiments. By explicitly representing the entities and relationships of the domain, the conceptual model provides knowledge that guides the definition of coherent feature subsets. Rather than replacing existing feature selection techniques, the proposed approach complements them by incorporating expert knowledge into the experimental design.

The approach is illustrated through a case study of Mohs micrographic surgery. The conceptual model is used to organize the variables into semantically meaningful groups that serve as the basis for different Machine Learning experiments.

Keywords: Conceptual Modeling · Machine Learning · Feature Selection · Mohs Micrographic Surgery

1 Introduction

Machine Learning (ML) has become one of the most widely adopted approaches for discovering predictive patterns from clinical data and supporting medical

F. M. Ferrer and E. N. Insa—These authors contributed equally to this work.

P. Fettke et al. (Eds.): ER 2026, LNCS 17125, pp. 20–35, 2027.
https://doi.org/10.1007/978-3-032-40377-3_2

decision-making [27]. Applications range from disease diagnosis and prognosis to treatment planning and personalized medicine, where predictive models exploit relationships among clinical variables to estimate outcomes of clinical interest [3]. Despite their success, the performance and generalization capability of ML models strongly depend on the quality, relevance, and representation of the input features [26].

In fact, in many biomedical applications, datasets are characterized by a limited number of samples together with a relatively large number of recorded variables. This high-dimensional, low-sample-size scenario increases the risk of overfitting and limits the ability of predictive models to generalize beyond the available data [6]. Consequently, reducing the dimensionality of the feature space has become a fundamental step in many ML pipelines. Feature Selection (FS) methods typically rely on statistical criteria or optimization algorithms to identify informative variables [2]. While these approaches are effective at reducing dimensionality, they generally evaluate variables according to statistical or predictive criteria rather than explicit domain semantics, potentially overlooking the conceptual relationships that exist among clinical concepts and the healthcare processes from which these variables originate [29].

This limitation is particularly relevant in healthcare. Clinical variables describe complementary aspects of patients, diseases, diagnostic procedures, treatments, and outcomes. Variables collected during different stages of the clinical process often represent related biomedical concepts whose meaning can only be fully understood within the context of the application domain. Consequently, selecting or grouping variables exclusively according to statistical criteria may produce feature sets that are difficult to interpret clinically or that fail to capture valuable domain knowledge. As a result, incorporating explicit domain knowledge into ML has become an increasingly active research area, particularly in biomedical applications where interpretability, transparency, and clinical validity are essential requirements [8,9].

In parallel, Conceptual Modeling (CM) offers a systematic mechanism for representing domain knowledge by explicitly describing the entities, relationships, and constraints that characterize a problem domain that is understandable by both domain experts and software engineers [20]. In the context of ML, this semantic layer can bridge the gap between clinical expertise and data-driven methods by making explicit how variables relate to the underlying concepts they represent. As a result, CM can support the definition of semantically coherent groups of variables, facilitating the design of more informed and transparent FS strategies while improving the interpretability of the overall experimental process.

This paper explores this idea through a case study of Mohs Micrographic Surgery (MMS), a tissue-sparing surgical technique considered the gold standard for the treatment of high-risk skin cancers due to its high cure rates and complete intraoperative margin assessment [10,28]. MMS is particularly advantageous for tumors with poorly defined clinical margins, where complete tumor removal must be balanced against maximal preservation of healthy tissue [15]. During the procedure, the tumor is removed in successive stages until histopathological examination confirms tumor-free margins [17,18,22]. However, accurately estimating the true subclinical extension of the tumor before surgery remains challenging, even when dermatoscopic and histopathological information is available, since tumor cells may extend beyond the clinically visible lesion [14,21]. Consequently, although many tumors are completely removed after a single stage, a considerable proportion require additional surgical stages because residual tumor cells remain after the initial excision [7,11,24,25]. The main objective of the case-study is to identify these cases preoperatively using patient-related and tumor-related variables, enabling dermatologic surgeons to plan the initial excision more accurately, reduce unnecessary surgical stages, and maximize the preservation of healthy tissue. The study was carried out in collaboration between the PROS Research Center and dermatologists from the Instituto Valenciano de Oncología (IVO).

The main contribution of this work is therefore a methodology that integrates CM into the feature engineering process. By explicitly representing domain semantics, the proposed approach supports semantically guided feature grouping, improves the transparency and reproducibility of experimental design, and strengthens the integration of clinical expertise into ML workflows.

This work is organized as follows: Sect. 2 reviews previous applications of CM and motivates its suitability for representing domain knowledge in biomedical scenarios. Section 3 explains the material and methods followed to develop the proposed approach. Section 4 presents the results of applying the approach to the MMS use case, in which a Conceptual Model for the domain is presented. Also, we present the separation of variables. Section 5 contains discussions of the results and Sect. 6 draws the main conclusions and future work.

2 Background of Conceptual Modeling

CM has been extensively adopted in Model-Driven Software Engineering as a mechanism for describing application domains independently of implementation details. It provides an explicit representation of domain entities, relationships, and constraints, enabling a shared understanding between domain experts and software engineers. This capability has been successfully exploited in the development of web applications [16] and in systems engineering, where conceptual models have been used to improve requirements specification and software quality [12].

Beyond software engineering, CM has also demonstrated its value in data-intensive scientific domains. In genomics, conceptual models have been proposed to organize the semantic complexity of genomic information and to support precision medicine applications by providing a structured representation of biological knowledge, facilitating the interpretation and management of highly heterogeneous datasets [5,13,19,23].

Similarly, CM has been increasingly adopted in medical informatics as a foundation for the development of clinical information systems. Recent proposals have employed CM to support the management, integration, and analysis of clinical data, as well as the generation of medical reports in domains such as ophthalmology and lung cancer diagnosis [1,4]. In these applications, CM improve communication between clinicians and software developers while providing a semantic organization of clinical information.

The semantic information encoded by conceptual representations has also been exploited beyond information system development. Recent research has investigated the use of semantic constraints to guide the selection of relevant information in data-driven tasks, demonstrating that incorporating domain semantics can improve the quality and interpretability of the selected information compared with purely data-driven approaches [30].

Unlike these previous works, which either use CM to support the development of information systems or exploit semantic knowledge in application-specific information selection processes, this paper investigates the use of CM as a mechanism for organizing the feature space of ML problems. Our hypothesis is that making domain knowledge explicit through a conceptual model enables the definition of semantically coherent groups of variables, providing a more informed basis for feature selection in small clinical datasets.

3 Material and Methods

The case study was based on a clinical data set, obtained from the IVO Melanoma Database, describing patient and tumor related characteristics. The methodological process combined clinical knowledge elicitation, systematic variable characterization, conceptual model construction to provide a semantic basis for the subsequent definition of feature subsets and application of CM to FS.

3.1 Knowledge Elicitation: Research Questions, Variable Characterization, and Semantic Grouping

The first stage of the methodology consisted of adquiring the clinical knowledge required to define the objectives of the case study and organize the available feature space. This process was conducted through a series of meetings with the dermatologists involved in the study. During these sessions, the clinical experts defined the research questions to be addressed, specified the clinical decisions that the predictive models were intended to support, and identified the variables considered potentially relevant to each objective.

Once the research questions had been established, each variable was systematically characterized according to its clinical meaning, source of acquisition, data type, and admissible domain of values. Variables were classified as binary, nominal categorical, ordinal categorical, or numerical. When applicable, their value domains were linked to established clinical terminologies or ontological concepts. Otherwise, they were represented using clinically meaningful categories or ranges defined by the experts at the time of data collection.

This characterization also distinguished between directly observed and clinically derived variables, as well as between variables describing the patient, the tumor, diagnostic assessments, tissue samples, and surgical procedures. In addition to supporting the subsequent CM process, the explicit representation of data types and value domains facilitated the exploratory data analysis, since several analytical procedures (such as correlation and univariate analyses) depend on the statistical nature of the variables.

Finally, the variables were organized into semantically coherent groups according to the clinical concepts they represented and their role within the MMS workflow. This semantic grouping provided a domain-informed structure for the feature space, allowing variables to be interpreted as related components of broader clinical concepts rather than as isolated predictors. The resulting groups were formally described in the conceptual model and used as the basis for the ML experiments.

3.2 Conceptual Model Construction

The information collected during the previous stages was formalized through the construction of a domain conceptual model. The modeling process began with the identification of the principal entities represented in the dataset. Particular attention was paid to the entity corresponding to the unit of analysis, since each observation in a ML dataset must represent a uniquely identifiable domain element. In this case study, each observation corresponded to a cutaneous tumor case associated with a patient and specific surgical procedures.

Once the main entities had been identified, their attributes, semantic relationships, and association cardinalities were defined. Each dataset variable was mapped to the entity and attribute that best represented its clinical meaning, rather than being modeled solely according to its position in the original data table. This process made it possible to distinguish variables describing the patient, the tumor, the preoperative assessment, the surgical procedure, and the resulting clinical outcome, while explicitly representing the relationships among these concepts.

The admissible values of each attribute were also formally represented in the conceptual schema. Binary variables were modeled using the *Boolean* data type, whereas numerical variables were represented using the *Float* data type. Categorical variables were modeled through explicitly defined enumerations, regardless of whether they were nominal or ordinal. For nominal variables, the enumeration specified the complete set of mutually exclusive categories without implying any intrinsic order. For ordinal variables, the enumeration additionally preserved the clinically meaningful ordering among categories. This representation made the value domain of each variable explicit and prevented categorical values from being interpreted as arbitrary numerical codes.

The use of enumerations also enabled the original dataset codifications to be replaced by semantically meaningful labels within the model. Consequently, each possible value could be interpreted directly by both clinical and technical experts, improving the transparency of the mapping between the dataset and the conceptual representation. Where applicable, enumeration values and numerical ranges were defined according to established clinical classifications, controlled terminologies, or expert-defined criteria.

The conceptual schema was expressed as a Unified Modeling Language (UML) class diagram and implemented using Visual Paradigm. The model was iteratively reviewed with the participating clinical experts. During each iteration, entities, attributes, relationships, cardinalities, data types, value domains, and enumeration values were assessed for semantic correctness, completeness, and clinical interpretability. The model was progressively refined until it adequately represented both the problem domain and the meaning of the variables included in the dataset.

3.3 Conceptual Model Applied to Feature Selection

The final conceptual model was used as the semantic backbone for defining the feature space of the ML experiments. For each research question, an initial set of potentially relevant variables had previously been identified in collaboration with the clinical experts, as described in Sect. 3.1. This initial selection delimited the variables considered clinically meaningful for addressing the corresponding objective.

These variables were subsequently organized according to the semantically coherent subsets defined by the conceptual model. Therefore, FS was not performed by assessing and selecting each variable independently. Instead, the subsets defined by the conceptual model were treated as the units of selection, and the groups considered most relevant to each research question were included in the corresponding ML analyses.

Consequently, variables were incorporated into or excluded from the models according to the domain concept to which they belonged, rather than solely on the basis of their individual statistical or predictive contribution. This group-based strategy introduces domain semantics into the feature-selection process, preserves the relationships among variables representing the same clinical concept, and makes the resulting experimental configurations more interpretable and traceable from both clinical and conceptual perspectives.

4 Results

In this section, we present the application of the methods described in Sect. 3 and their outcome.

4.1 Research Questions, Variable Characterization and Semantic Variable Groups

The clinical knowledge elicitation and variable characterization stages resulted in the definition of three research questions and seven semantically coherent groups of variables.

The primary research question was formulated as follows:

Can the number of surgical stages required to achieve complete tumor excision be predicted from the available patient- and tumor-related variables?

This research question aimed to identify the sources of clinical information associated with the complexity of the MMS procedure, as reflected by the number of stages required to achieve tumor-free margins. For this objective, no semantic variable group was excluded *a priori*, since variables collected throughout the clinical and surgical workflow could contribute relevant information.

The second research question was formulated as follows:

Can the presence of a specific tumor mutation be predicted from the remaining patient- and tumor-related variables?

For this research question, no semantic variable group was excluded *a priori*. Each mutation was considered separately as a binary prediction target. Accordingly, the mutation being predicted was removed from its corresponding predictor set to prevent target leakage, whereas the remaining variables were retained as candidate predictors, except for the other mutations.

The third research question was formulated as follows:

Can tumor Breslow thickness be predicted using information available before the first surgical excision?

This research question aimed to support preoperative planning, since Breslow thickness influences the surgical management of the tumor. Consequently, only variables available before the first excision were considered as candidate predictors. Variables obtained from the histological examination of the first excision were excluded *a priori*, as they would not be available at the intended time of prediction. In addition, any variable directly encoding the target Breslow thickness was removed from the predictor set to prevent information leakage.

The characterization of the available variables according to their clinical meaning, source of acquisition, and value domain resulted in the following semantic groups:

- **Patient demographic variables:** *age*, represented as a discrete numerical variable; *sex*, represented as a binary variable; and *skin phototype*, represented as an ordinal categorical variable.
- **Tumor clinical variables:** *tumor location*, represented as a categorical variable; *tumor diameter*, represented as a continuous numerical variable; *tumor color*, represented as a categorical variable; *clinical tumor borders*, represented as a binary variable distinguishing between well-defined and poorly defined borders; *and tumor presentation*, represented as a binary variable distinguishing between primary and recurrent tumors.
- **Tumor dermatoscopic variables:** *annular-granular pattern*, *asymmetric follicular openings*, *rhomboidal structures*, and *follicular obliteration*. Each dermatoscopic feature was represented as a binary variable indicating its presence or absence.

- **Biopsy histological variables:** *pagetoid spread*, *nesting*, *inflamation of the tumor*, *solar elastosis*, *melanocyte pigmentation*, and *involvement of adnexal epithelia*, represented as ordinal categorical variables; *CSD*, *subepidermal clefting*, *melanocytes arranged in rows*, *multinucleated melanocytes*, and *melanophages*, represented as binary variables indicating their presence or absence; *predominant melanocyte type* and *Clark level*, represented as categorical variables; and *Breslow thickness*, represented as a continuous numerical variable.
- **Biopsy mutation variables:** mutations in *BRAF*, *NRAS*, *C-KIT*, and *TERT*, each represented as a binary variable indicating the presence or absence of the corresponding mutation.
- **First-excision histological variables:** *pagetoid spread*, *nesting*, *inflamation of the tumor*, *solar elastosis*, *melanocyte pigmentation*, and *involvement of adnexal epithelia*, represented as ordinal categorical variables; *CSD*, *subepidermal clefting*, *melanocytes arranged in rows*, *multinucleated melano-cytes*, and *melanophages*, represented as binary variables indicating their presence or absence; *predominant melanocyte type* and *Clark level*, represented as categorical variables; and *Breslow thickness*, represented as a continuous numerical variable.
- **Tumor surgical variables:** the number of *surgical stages* required to reach complete tumor excision, represented as a discrete numerical variable.

These groups provided the semantic structure from which the domain entities, attributes, value domains, and relationships of the conceptual model were derived. The resulting conceptual representation is presented in the following subsection.

4.2 Conceptual Model of the Mohs Micrographic Surgery Domain

Based on the knowledge elicited from the domain experts, a conceptual model was developed to provide an explicit semantic representation of the clinical domain under study. The complete model is presented in Fig. 1. As described in Sect. 3.2, its construction followed a systematic and iterative process in which the relevant domain entities, their attributes, the relationships between them, and the corresponding cardinalities were progressively identified and refined through repeated reviews and consultations with the participating dermatologists.

During this process, categorical variables were identified and represented as UML enumeration classes. This modeling decision makes the admissible values of each categorical attribute explicit and replaces potentially ambiguous dataset codes with semantically meaningful categories. Nominal enumerations define sets of categories without an intrinsic order, whereas ordinal enumerations preserve the clinically meaningful ordering between their possible values. This representation increases the interpretability of the conceptual model and facilitates the traceability between the original dataset and the clinical concepts represented within it.

The conceptual model is described below through a fictitious use case involving a patient undergoing MMS. This example illustrates the clinical and data-generation workflow represented by the model. In parallel, the different views superimposed on the conceptual model delimit the semantic variable groups defined in the previous subsection, as shown in Fig. 2.

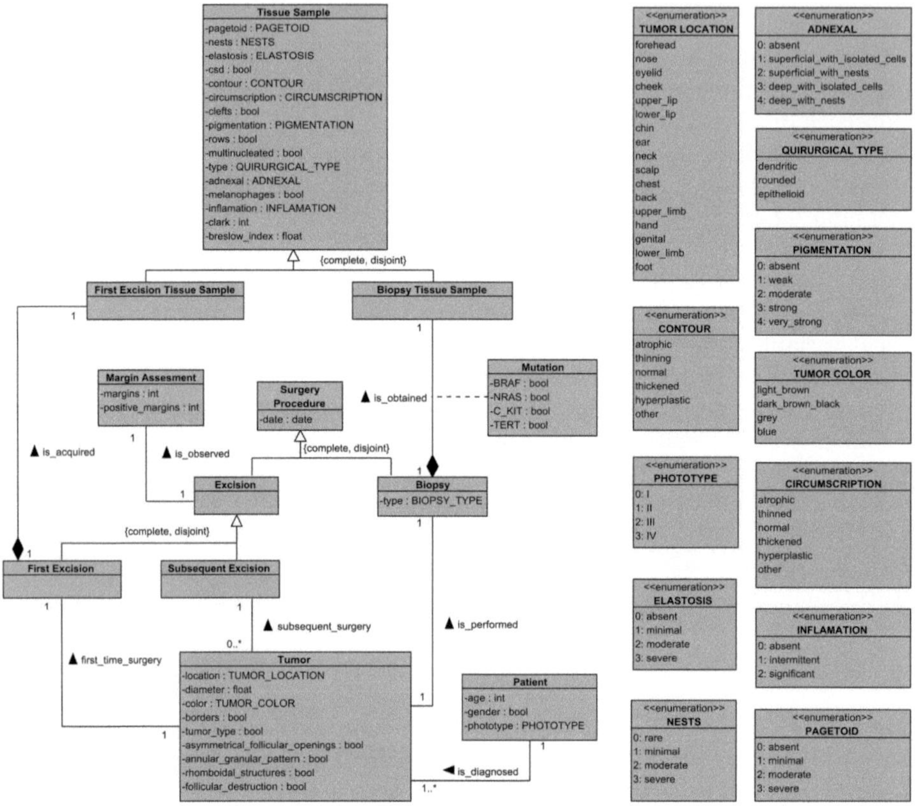

Fig. 1. Conceptual model of the MMS.

The workflow begins with a patient, represented by the *Patient* entity. Each patient is described by demographic attributes, including age, sex, and phototype. These attributes constitute the patient demographic variables group.

A patient may be diagnosed with one or more cutaneous tumors requiring MMS. Each lesion is represented by the *Tumor* entity, which constitutes the central entity of the conceptual model and the unit of analysis represented by each observation in the dataset. The relationship between *Patient* and *Tumor* captures the fact that a patient may present multiple tumors, whereas each tumor is associated with a specific patient.

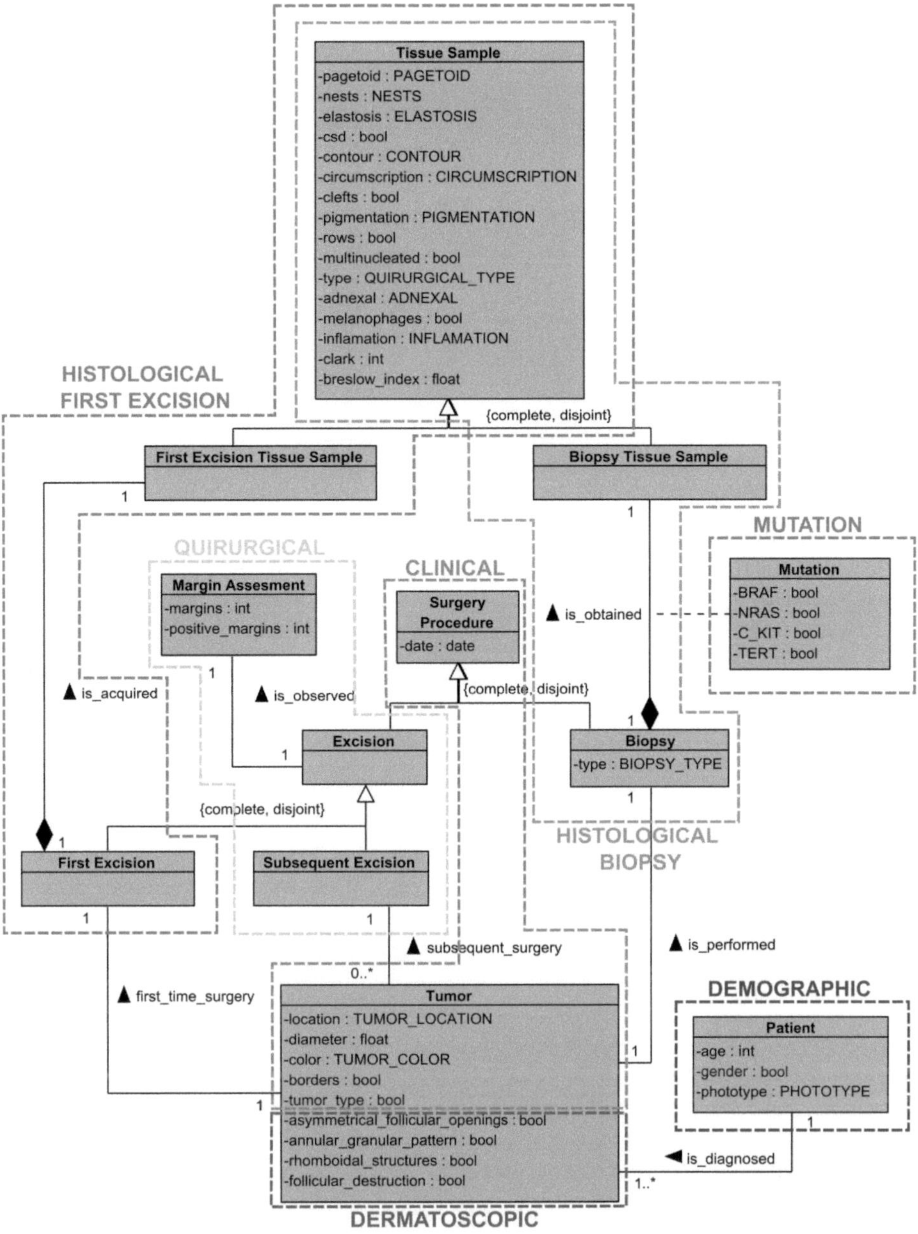

Fig. 2. View of the conceptual model by variable groups, without enumerations.

Each tumor is initially characterized through clinical variables describing its macroscopic appearance and clinical presentation. These attributes include tumor color, anatomical location, diameter, tumor presentation as primary or recurrent, and whether its clinical borders are well or poorly defined. Together, these attributes constitute the tumor clinical variables group.

The tumor may also be examined by dermoscopy, providing a more detailed characterization of structures that may not be identifiable through unaided visual examination. The dermoscopic attributes represented in the model record the presence or absence of an annular-granular pattern, asymmetric follicular openings, rhomboidal structures, and follicular obliteration. These attributes constitute the tumor dermoscopic variables group.

Once the tumor has been diagnosed, a biopsy procedure is performed to obtain a representative tissue specimen. Tissue specimens are represented through the general *Tissue Sample* entity. The sample collected during the diagnostic biopsy is represented by the specialized entity *Biopsy Tissue Sample*. This specialization distinguishes the partial specimen obtained before surgery from the tissue removed during the subsequent surgical excision.

The biopsy tissue sample is examined microscopically to obtain its histopathological characteristics. These observations generate the biopsy histological variables group, which includes pagetoid spread, nesting, solar elastosis, CSD, subepidermal clefting, melanocytes arranged in rows, melanocyte pigmentation, multinucleated melanocytes, predominant melanocyte type, involvement of adnexal epithelia, melanophages, Clark level, and Breslow thickness.

The biopsy tissue sample may also undergo molecular analysis to determine the presence or absence of the genetic alterations included in the study. The resulting information constitutes the mutation variables group, which records the mutational status of *BRAF*, *NRAS*, *C-KIT*, and *TERT*.

After the biopsy has been performed and assessed, the patient is scheduled for MMS. The clinical workflow records both the biopsy date and the date of the first excision. These temporal attributes allow the interval between the biopsy and the first surgical excision to be calculated. This derived temporal variable completes the clinical variables group.

MMS is represented as a surgical procedure composed of one or more successive excisions. The general concept of an excision is represented by the *Excision* entity. Within this hierarchy, the first excision is modeled as a specialization because detailed histological information was collected specifically from the tissue removed during the first surgical stage.

During the first excision, the clinically identified tumor is removed and the resulting tissue specimen is examined microscopically. This examination generates the first-excision histological variables group. In the model, the specimen is a specialization of the *Tissue Sample*, called *First Excision Tissue Sample*, similar to the biopsy one.

Following each excision, the surgical margins are examined to determine whether residual neoplastic tissue remains. If the margins are not free of tumor, an additional Mohs stage is performed, producing a subsequent excision whose margins are again assessed. This iterative process continues until complete tumor removal is confirmed.

Each excision is therefore associated with its corresponding surgical stage and margin assessment. Once tumor-free margins have been achieved, the total number of stages required to complete the procedure is recorded. The number of surgical stages, together with the information obtained from the successive margin assessments, constitutes the surgical variables group.

The resulting conceptual model provides an integrated representation of the complete data workflow, from the demographic characterization of the patient and the preoperative assessment of the tumor to the biopsy analyses, the successive surgical excisions, and the final surgical outcome. This semantic organization provides the basis for the subsequent application of the conceptual model to the ML experiments.

4.3 Conceptual Model-Guided Feature Selection

The semantic views defined over the conceptual model were used as the units of FS for the three research questions. Therefore, the experimental process did not select variables independently. Instead, variables were included in the ML models according to the conceptual view to which they belonged, preserving their clinical meaning, provenance, and relationships with other variables describing the same domain concept.

For each research question, the views that were compatible with the corresponding prediction scenario were first identified. All admissible combinations of these views were then systematically evaluated. Each combination defined a different feature space containing all the variables associated with the selected views. These feature-space configurations were evaluated across the candidate ML algorithms to identify the combination of semantic views and model that achieved the best predictive performance.

For the first research question, which aimed to predict the number of surgical stages required to achieve complete tumor excision (number of total excisions, in the model), the candidate feature space comprised the following conceptual-model views:

- *Clinical Data, Demographic Data, Dermatoscopic Data, Histological Data from biopsy, Histological Data from first excision and Mutation Data.*

For the second research question, a separate binary prediction problem was defined for each assessed mutation. The mutation considered as the target in each experiment was excluded from the predictor space to prevent target leakage. The remaining candidate views were:

- *Clinical Data, Demographic Data, Dermatoscopic Data, Histological Data from biopsy, Histological Data from first excision and Surgical Data.*

For the third research question, which aimed to predict tumor Breslow thickness before the first surgical excision (breslow index in the model), only views containing information available at the intended time of prediction were considered. Accordingly, the candidate feature space included:

– *Clinical Data, Demographic Data, Dermatoscopic Data, Histological Data from biopsy (without breslow index) and Mutation Data.*

All admissible combinations of the eligible conceptual-model views and candidate ML algorithms were systematically evaluated for each research question and target variable. This exhaustive search enabled the identification of both the best-performing model and the optimal combination of semantic feature groups. Since the contribution of the different variable views was assessed by comparing models in which specific groups were included or excluded, this procedure can be regarded as an ablation-style analysis.

5 Discussion

The results of this case study illustrate how CM can introduce domain semantics into the FS process. Instead of representing the dataset as an unstructured collection of predictors, the proposed methodology formally contextualizes the clinical problem and organizes the variables according to the patient, tumor, diagnostic, histological, molecular, and surgical concepts to which they belong. This representation improves the traceability between the clinical workflow, the available data, and the feature spaces evaluated in the ML experiments.

The use of semantically coherent variable groups also makes the systematic exploration of alternative feature spaces computationally feasible. If all variables were selected independently, the number of possible combinations would increase exponentially with the number of predictors, making an exhaustive evaluation impractical. By treating the conceptual model views as the units of selection, the search space depends on the substantially smaller number of semantic groups. This enables the joint exploration of different group combinations and ML algorithms to identify both the most suitable model and the most informative sources of clinical information for each research question.

This group-based strategy is particularly relevant in clinical datasets with a limited number of observations. Reducing the dimensionality of the feature space may help limit model complexity and the risk of overfitting. At the same time, selecting complete semantic groups preserves the relationships among variables describing the same clinical concept, avoiding a reduction process based exclusively on isolated statistical associations. Consequently, dimensionality can be reduced without completely sacrificing clinical interpretability or domain context.

An additional advantage is that the resulting models can be interpreted at two complementary levels. Individual predictors may still be examined within each model, while the selected views indicate which broader clinical domains contribute relevant information to the prediction task. This provides an explanation that is potentially more meaningful to domain experts than a list of independently selected variables.

Nevertheless, the approach depends on the quality and completeness of the conceptual model and on the knowledge elicited from the participating experts.

Moreover, selecting variables at the group level may retain predictors with limited individual contribution or exclude potentially useful variables belonging to a less informative group. Therefore, conceptual model based selection should be regarded as a semantic complement to conventional statistical and model based FS techniques rather than as a complete replacement for them.

6 Conclusions and Future Work

This work has explored the integration of CM as a semantic framework to guide feature selection in ML workflows, specifically targeting clinical scenarios characterized by limited sample sizes and numerous variables.

6.1 Conclusions and Contributions

The main conclusion of this article is that incorporating domain knowledge through explicit conceptual schemas significantly enhances the experimental design of ML pipelines. The proposed approach maintains full semantic interpretability. By organizing variables into fixed, coherent conceptual groups based on the underlying entities and relationships of the domain, we ensure that subsequent FS processes yield results that are both statistically valuable and clinically explainable.

As a main contribution, a formalized domain schema has been developed in collaboration with dermatologists from the IVO. This model successfully serves as a semantic backbone to organize the feature space for predictive modeling by enabling a clear semantic separation of the variable groups involved.

6.2 Future Work

We plan to validate the generalizability of the methodology by applying it to other clinical use cases and different medical or surgical domains characterized by distinct workflows and data constraints. Furthermore, we aim to enhance the construction of the conceptual models by shifting from the ad-hoc elicitation criteria of domain professionals toward the integration of standardized biomedical ontologies and controlled terminologies. This evolution will automate part of the semantic mapping process and ensure broader interoperability and standardization across heterogeneous healthcare datasets.

Acknowledgements. The authors would like to thank the PROS Research Group of the VRAIN Research Institute of the UPV for their valuable discussions on the CM, as well as the dermatologists of the Instituto Valenciano de Oncología to facilitating our work and enhancing our understanding of the domain.

This work is part of the Horizon Europe project BETTER, funded by the European Union's Horizon Europe research and innovation program under grant agreement No. 101136262.

References

1. Carreño-Bolufer, J., Reyes Román, J.F., Cabrera Beyrouti, R., Casamayor Ródenas, J.C.: Agc-mac: a conceptual model-based platform for the management and analysis of clinical data of retina-macula diseases. In: International Conference on Web Engineering, pp. 65–76. Springer, Heidelberg (2024). https://doi.org/10.1007/978-3-031-75110-3_6
2. Chandrashekar, G., Sahin, F.: A survey on feature selection methods. Comput. Electr. Eng. **40**(1), 16–28 (2014)
3. Esteva, A., et al.: A guide to deep learning in healthcare. Nat. Med. **25**(1), 24–29 (2019)
4. Ferrer, F.M., Román, J.F.R., Sánchez, P.A., Carreño-Bolufer, J., Calabuig, E.C., Pastor, O.: A conceptual model-based platform for semi-automatic report generation to streamline medical diagnostics of lung cancer and pet/ct data management. In: MODELSWARD, pp. 418–425 (2026)
5. García, A., Palacio, A.L., Roman, J.F.R., Casamayor, J.C., Pastor, O.: A conceptual model-based approach to improve the representation and management of omics data in precision medicine. IEEE Access **9**, 154071–154085 (2021)
6. Hastie, T., Tibshirani, R., Friedman, J.: The elements of statistical learning (2009)
7. Hilari, H., et al.: Conventional surgery compared with slow mohs micrographic surgery in the treatment of lentigo maligna: a retrospective study of 62 cases. Actas Dermo-Sifiliográficas (English Edition) **103**(7), 614–623 (2012)
8. Holzinger, A., Biemann, C., Pattichis, C.S., Kell, D.B.: What do we need to build explainable ai systems for the medical domain? arXiv preprint arXiv:1712.09923 (2017)
9. Holzinger, A., Langs, G., Denk, H., Zatloukal, K., Müller, H.: Causability and explainability of artificial intelligence in medicine. Wiley Interdisc. Rev. Data Mining Knowl. Disc. **9**(4), e1312 (2019)
10. Kasprzak, J.M., Xu, Y.G.: Diagnosis and management of lentigo maligna: a review. Drugs Context **4**, 212281 (2015)
11. Kunishige, J.H., Doan, L., Brodland, D.G., Zitelli, J.A.: Comparison of surgical margins for lentigo maligna versus melanoma in situ. J. Am. Acad. Dermatol. **81**(1), 204–212 (2019)
12. Le Pors, E., Grisvard, O.: Conceptual modeling for system requirements enhancement. In: Kordon, F., Kermarrec, Y. (eds.) Ada-Europe 2009. LNCS, vol. 5570, pp. 251–265. Springer, Heidelberg (2009). https://doi.org/10.1007/978-3-642-01924-1_18
13. Martínez-Minguet, D., Pastor, Ó.: Conceptual modeling for polygenic risk score research: improving domain understanding and clinical utility. In: Saeki, M., et al. (eds.) Advances in Conceptual Modeling, pp. 159–168. Springer, Cham (2025). https://doi.org/10.1007/978-3-031-75599-6_12
14. Massi, G., LeBoit, P.E.: Histological Diagnosis of Nevi and Melanoma. Springer, Heidelberg (2013). https://doi.org/10.1007/978-3-642-37311-4
15. McGuire, L.K., Disa, J.J., Lee, E.H., Busam, K.J., Nehal, K.S.: Melanoma of the lentigo maligna subtype: diagnostic challenges and current treatment paradigms. Plast. Reconstr. Surg. **129**(2), 288e–299e (2012)
16. Meliá, S., Gomez, J.: The websa approach: applying model driven engineering to web applications. J. Web Eng. 121–149 (2006)
17. Moreno, A., et al.: Histologic features associated with an invasive component in lentigo maligna lesions. JAMA Dermatol. **155**(7), 782–788 (2019)

18. Moro, R., et al.: May melanophages hinder the subclinical spread of lentigo maligna and lentigo maligna melanoma? Results from a pilot study. J. Eur. Acad. Dermatol. Venereol. **35**(6) (2021)
19. Palacio, A.L., López, Ó.P., Ródenas, J.C.C.: A method to identify relevant genome data: conceptual modeling for the medicine of precision. In: Trujillo, J.C., et al. (eds.) ER 2018. LNCS, vol. 11157, pp. 597–609. Springer, Cham (2018). https://doi.org/10.1007/978-3-030-00847-5_44
20. Pastor, O., Molina, J.C.: Model-Driven Architecture in Practice: A Software Production Environment Based on Conceptual Modeling. Springer, Heidelberg (2007). https://doi.org/10.1007/978-3-540-71868-0_7
21. Pellacani, G., et al.: The smart approach: feasibility of lentigo maligna superficial margin assessment with hand-held reflectance confocal microscopy technology. J. Eur. Acad. Dermatol. Venereol. **32**(10), 1687–1694 (2018)
22. Requena, C., Manrique, E., Nagore, E.: [translated article] update on lentigo maligna: diagnostic signs and treatment. Actas Dermo-Sifiliograficas **114**(5), T413–T424 (2023)
23. Reyes Román, J.F., Pastor, Ó., Casamayor, J.C., Valverde, F.: Applying conceptual modeling to better understand the human genome. In: Comyn-Wattiau, I., Tanaka, K., Song, I.-Y., Yamamoto, S., Saeki, M. (eds.) ER 2016. LNCS, vol. 9974, pp. 404–412. Springer, Cham (2016). https://doi.org/10.1007/978-3-319-46397-1_31
24. Shin, T.M., et al.: Clinical factors associated with subclinical spread of in situ melanoma. J. Am. Acad. Dermatol. **76**(4), 707–713 (2017)
25. Shin, T.M., et al.: Clinical and pathologic factors associated with subclinical spread of invasive melanoma. J. Am. Acad. Dermatol. **76**(4), 714–721 (2017)
26. Soni, A., Arora, C., Kaushik, R., Upadhyay, V.: Evaluating the impact of data quality on machine learning model performance. J. Nonlinear Anal. Optim **14**(01), 13–18 (2023)
27. Topol, E.J.: High-performance medicine: the convergence of human and artificial intelligence. Nat. Med. **25**(1), 44–56 (2019)
28. Tzellos, T., Kyrgidis, A., Mocellin, S., Chan, A.W., Pilati, P., Apalla, Z.: Interventions for melanoma in situ, including lentigo maligna. Cochrane Database Syst. Rev. (12) (2014)
29. Von Rueden, L., et al.: Informed machine learning-a taxonomy and survey of integrating prior knowledge into learning systems. IEEE Trans. Knowl. Data Eng. **35**(1), 614–633 (2021)
30. Zhu, Q., et al.: Semantics-constrained advantageous information selection of multimodal spatiotemporal data for landslide disaster assessment. ISPRS Int. J. Geo Inf. **8**(2), 68 (2019)

LLM4Modeling

Copy That? The Influence of Process Model Representation Format on LLM Comprehension

Fabian Rybinski(✉), Nadja Kruse, Adrian Wilhelm, and Andreas Fritsch

Karlsruhe Institute of Technology (KIT), Karlsruhe, Germany
{fabian.rybinski,nadja.kruse,andreas.fritsch}@kit.edu

Abstract. LLMs are increasingly applied across the business process management (BPM) lifecycle, e.g., for analyzing or documenting processes. How reliably they support these applications depends on how well they comprehend the underlying process model. In practice, the same process model may be provided to an LLM in different ways, e.g., as a structured serialization or a rendered diagram. However, it is unclear whether and to what extent the choice of representation format affects comprehension. We address this gap with a systematic study that assesses comprehension through interpretation quality, i.e., the graded correctness of task responses. We compare the representation formats of the same process model in three categories: natural-language text, rendered diagrams, and structured serializations. This yields four isolated formats (textual narrative, PNG, BPMN-XML, Mermaid) and selected hybrid combinations, all derived from a common set of BPMN models. We evaluate these format configurations across six LLMs, eight processes, and eleven task types. An LLM-as-a-judge scores responses against reference answers using a graded metric and an error taxonomy. The results show that the representation format substantially affects interpretation quality, with no single format being best across all LLMs. The isolated PNG is consistently the weakest, while hybrid combinations of natural-language text with BPMN-XML or Mermaid emerge as the strongest formats overall. These findings establish the representation format as a design variable for LLM-supported BPM tasks and yield implications for its selection.

Keywords: Process Model Comprehension · Process Model Representation · Large Language Models

1 Introduction

Large language models (LLMs) are increasingly applied across the business process management (BPM) lifecycle, where their ability to produce context-aware responses and convert unstructured input into structured representations makes them attractive assistants, most visibly for generating process models

P. Fettke et al. (Eds.): ER 2026, LNCS 17125, pp. 39–56, 2027.
https://doi.org/10.1007/978-3-032-40377-3_3

from natural-language text [18]. However, generating a process model is only one part of the lifecycle. The reliability of LLM support for modeling, improving, and analyzing process models depends on how well the LLM comprehends the model that a given representation format describes. Process comprehension is thus a foundational capability for LLM support across the BPM lifecycle. It is also what allows LLMs to make process knowledge accessible to stakeholders regardless of their modeling background [10]. Realizing this potential requires coping with the heterogeneity of how process knowledge is represented. In organizations, the content of a process model can be documented as a natural-language text, a rendered diagram in a modeling notation, or in structured serializations. In principle, multimodal LLMs (mLLMs) can ingest all of these formats, as well as hybrids that combine them [14]. It is therefore an open question which representation format is best suited as the input for an LLM.

Just as research on human process model comprehension shows that the way a model is presented influences how well it is understood [7,21], we expect the representation format to influence how well LLMs interpret a process model. Existing work on LLM in BPM has focused primarily on process model generation [15], leaving open whether and to what extent the format affects the interpretation quality of LLMs, and whether such an effect varies across different types of comprehension tasks. To address this, the study is structured around three research questions.

- **RQ1**: To what extent does the representation format of a process model affect the interpretation quality of LLMs?
- **RQ2**: How does this effect interact with LLM characteristics such as model size?
- **RQ3**: Which representation formats suit which types of comprehension tasks?

To answer these questions, we conduct a systematic study that crosses nine representation formats with six LLMs, eight processes of varying control-flow complexity, and eleven comprehension task types. These tasks operationalize comprehension at different levels, ranging from identifying structural elements and interpreting control-flow logic to validating execution traces and summarizing the process. To study the process comprehension of LLMs, we measure the interpretation quality by grading the correctness of LLM responses. All artifacts are grounded in a common set of Business Process Model and Notation (BPMN) models from which we derive four isolated representation formats and selected hybrid combinations. A semi-automated pipeline with an LLM-as-a-judge yields 16,632 judged responses.

Overall, the paper makes three main contributions. First, we provide a systematic evaluation that varies the representation format while keeping the process model content constant, so that observed differences can be attributed to the format rather than the content. Second, we introduce an evaluation approach that supports semantic assessment and can be reused to benchmark future LLMs under identical conditions. Third, we derive practice-oriented implications for selecting representation formats in LLM-supported BPM applications.

The remainder of the paper is organized as follows. Section 2 introduces the necessary background on process model representation formats. Section 3 reviews related work on LLMs for process analysis and positions our study against it. Section 4 details the study design. Section 5 reports the results, which Sect. 6 discusses together with their implications for modeling theory and practice. Section 7 concludes the paper.

2 Background

2.1 Process Models and Model Comprehension

A business process is a set of coordinated activities carried out to achieve a particular goal. A process model is its explicit representation, capturing the activities, their execution order, and the conditions under which they occur [7]. Such models act as a shared artifact for communication, analysis, and automation throughout the process lifecycle. However, their value depends on how well they can be understood. Research on process model comprehension shows that the format in which a process is presented measurably affects how readers interpret it [7,21]. Research treats comprehension as a latent construct that must be inferred from performance on questions about the model content. Building on human learning, [11] distinguishes surface-level comprehension from deeper understanding that requires inferences beyond the presented content. [27] further describes that the comparison of representations is only interpretable when the informational content is held constant across the compared representations. Later work shows that comprehension emerges from the interplay of a representation's semantics and its pragmatics [1], and empirical studies assess how specific representation choices affect it [8,26]. We adopt this terminology and the question-based approach and transfer the role of the model reader to an LLM.

2.2 Process Modeling Languages

Process modeling languages range from Petri nets to UML activity diagrams [22]. Among them, BPMN has become the de-facto standard in practice [25]. While the BPMN specification comprises many elements, its core constructs are events, activities, gateways, sequence flows, pools and lanes denoting responsibilities. The processes in this study are based on this core subset [25]. The standard also defines an XML serialization as the interchange format between modeling tools [25].

2.3 Process Model Representation Formats

The content of a process model can be represented in fundamentally different formats without changing the underlying process logic. A distinction must be drawn between representing a process itself and representing a process model. The formats compared in this study are representations of the same process model, whereas representations of the process itself would correspond to alternative modeling languages, which may capture different aspects of a process. Based on the classification of inputs that mLLMs can process [14], we distinguish three categories of representation formats

Natural-Language Text: A description written in prose, e.g., work instructions or interview transcripts. As the concrete format, we use a textual narrative that is an idealized description verbalizing the process model content. It is the most accessible form for non-experts, but it leaves control flow implicit and can be ambiguous, as natural language may admit more than one reading of the same description.

Rendered Diagram: The graphical process diagram, i.e., the rendered model shown in a modeling tool, exported as a PNG image. It makes control flow explicit through nodes and connectors. It is an image and therefore requires visual interpretation.

Structured Serialization: A machine-readable, text-based serialization that encodes model elements and their relations in a defined syntax. We consider two formats that mark opposite ends of verbosity: BPMN-XML, the standard interchange format, whose markup is highly verbose and Mermaid [29], a lightweight, text-based diagram syntax widely used in diagram-as-code settings. Mermaid encodes the same structure as BPMN-XML but is far more concise.

Hybrid Formats: A combination of two isolated formats from different categories, mirroring common practice where process documentation combines explanatory prose with a diagram or an underlying process model file.

2.4 Large Language Models

LLMs are neural language models based on the transformer architecture, trained on large text corpora to predict and generate language, operated through prompting without task-specific retraining [31]. Reasoning LLMs additionally produce explicit intermediate reasoning steps before the final answer, aiding multi-step inference [19]. mLLMs can also process non-textual input such as images [14]. LLMs are available as open-weight or proprietary models.

3 Related Work

We situate our work within two strands of research: LLMs for process analysis, and the impact of representation formats.

LLMs for Process Model Generation and Analysis. Previous research on LLMs in BPM has primarily targeted process model generation, converting natural-language descriptions into graphical models such as BPMN models or Petri nets, either through pipelines that chain multiple LLMs or through iterative model construction via conversational interfaces [9,18]. This aligns with the broader vision of process-aware assistants that combine LLMs with process knowledge [15]. More recently, LLMs have been applied to a range of process analysis and process mining tasks [2,12]. However, these studies typically use a single, fixed representation and they assess whether LLMs produce useful end results rather than isolating how well the LLM interprets the process model in the first place.

Representation Formats as a Variable. A smaller but growing body of work examines the representation format as an explanatory variable. [17] develop AIPA, a conversational assistant for process querying, and compare four abstractions of BPMN models as LLM inputs. They use three structured serializations (XML, a simplified XML, and JSON) and a PNG rendering, in order to configure this assistant. Their findings show that the image format lags behind overall and that effectiveness depends on question type and process complexity. Their evaluation proceeds sequentially: the four formats are compared on a single LLM (GPT-4o), the format with the best quality-to-token trade-off (simplified XML) is fixed, and four large LLMs are then compared on that format only.

Other studies touch representation format effects without isolating them for comprehension. [4] compare representation formats, but for process model generation, and provide the corresponding PMo dataset [3] that we build on. [6] explore multimodal BPMN analysis, yet at limited scale and without holding the model content constant across formats, so that representation and content effects remain confounded. Beyond BPM, vision-language research shows that input modality strongly affects diagram understanding [30]. However, these studies target generic flowcharts.

Further related work examines representation effects for conceptual models that complement the process perspective. Comparing PlantUML and JSON serializations of UML class diagrams, [23] find that the more compact PlantUML consistently outperforms JSON, with accuracy degrading as context size grows. However, the findings stem from structural models, restricted to two textual serializations and QA tasks, and the authors note that diagram types with behavioral semantics may interact differently with LLMs.

Positioning Our Study. The closest work to ours is that of [17], yet it answers a different question. For them, the format comparison is one configuration step in building an assistant. The format effect itself is not the research object. A sequential method, which selects the best format on one LLM and then compares LLMs on that format only, presupposes that a format ranking obtained for one LLM and one task can be transferred to other LLMs and tasks. Whether this premise holds is precisely our research question. Testing this requires a fully crossed design like the one we employ: nine format configurations, including the natural-language narrative and hybrid formats absent from their comparison, crossed with eleven task types and seven LLM configurations. A further methodological differentiation is that they use GPT-4o to score outputs that partly stem from GPT-4o itself, a setup susceptible to self-preference bias [32]. In our experimental setup, the judge is not among the evaluated configurations and applies a calibrated graded metric with an error taxonomy.

4 Study Design

4.1 Research Design

The study follows a controlled design in which the representation format is the independent variable and interpretation quality is the dependent variable. Following established practice in process model comprehension [21], we treat comprehension as a latent construct and operationalize it as interpretation quality: the graded correctness of an LLM's responses to comprehension tasks, assessed against reference answers. This follows the question-based measurement tradition of conceptual-model comprehension research (Sect. 2.1). In line with [27], all compared formats are informationally equivalent representations of the same model content. The design crosses four dimensions: eight processes of varying control-flow complexity, nine representation formats, eleven comprehension task types, and seven LLM configurations. Each of the resulting $8 \times 11 \times 9 \times 7 = 5{,}544$ task instances is issued in three iterations to dampen the effect of LLM nondeterminism, yielding 16,632 responses, each scored by an LLM-as-a-judge.

4.2 Process Dataset and Selection

We draw processes from the PMo [3] dataset, a curated collection of 55 BPMN models providing each process model in multiple representation formats. For each process, BPMN-XML serves as the ground truth from which all other formats are derived, maintaining consistent process model content across representation formats. The dataset uses a reduced BPMN notation subset: standard tasks; basic events; exclusive, parallel, inclusive gateways; sequence, message flows; pools, lanes. We select eight processes based on control-flow complexity (CFC), which quantifies the states induced by branching [5]. Table 1 summarizes the selection.

Table 1. Selected process models from PMo, ordered by CFC.

ID	Selection rationale	CFC
27	Maximum control-flow complexity within the dataset	21
18	High complexity, pronounced sequential depth without pool or lane structure	19
17	High gateway density relative to the total number of elements	14
32	Elevated complexity, modeled across multiple lanes to probe visual capture	13
44	Moderate complexity, heterogeneous task types	8
38	Inclusion of special modeling elements (collapsed pools)	7
21	Low complexity, lanes within a single pool	6
50	Minimal complexity, few nodes and edges	2

4.3 Representation Formats

From each BPMN model, we derive the four isolated representation formats introduced in Sect. 2.3: the *textual narrative*, a natural-language text slightly adapted from PMo; the *PNG*, the process model rendered as an image; *BPMN-XML*, the standard XML serialization; and *Mermaid*, a concise text-based diagram syntax covering the compact end of the serialization category. Based on these, we include hybrid formats pairing two isolated formats from different categories, yielding nine representation formats in total: four isolated and five hybrid combinations (Fig. 1).

PNG diagram

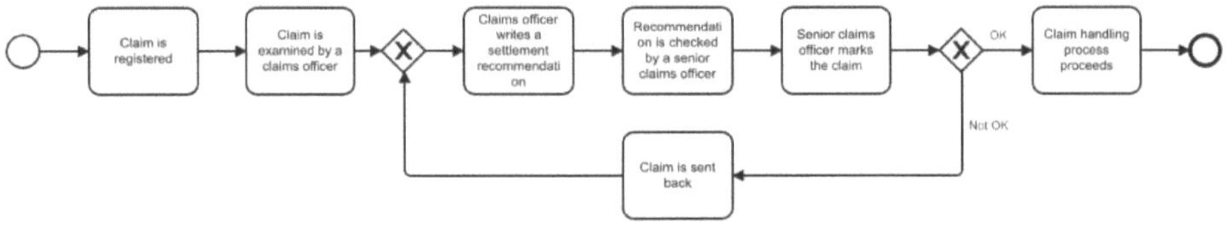

Textual narrative (excerpt)

After a claim is registered, it is examined by a claims officer. [...] If the claim is OK, the claim handling process proceeds.

BPMN-XML (excerpt)

```
<task id="Task_1"
  name="Claim is registered">
 <outgoing>SequenceFlow_2
      </outgoing>
</task> <!-- ... -->
```

Mermaid (excerpt)

```
graph LR
 S((" ")) --> T1["Claim is
   registered"]
 T1 --> T2["..."]
```

Fig. 1. The four isolated representation formats, illustrated for one process of the study (claim handling). Hybrid formats pair two formats from different categories.

4.4 Large Language Models

We selected various multimodal LLMs with sufficient context windows. Within these constraints, we vary model scale, provider, license model (open weight vs. proprietary), and training (instruct vs. reasoning). Table 2 lists the resulting selection of six LLMs, current as of the selection cutoff of 1 February 2026. GPT-5.2 is evaluated in two reasoning configurations (medium and none), yielding seven LLM configurations in total.

4.5 Comprehension Tasks

We define eleven task types inspired by process model comprehension categories relevant to our LLM context [24], trace validation and next-step prediction tasks adapted from [28], and the summarization questions of [2]. Seven of them are question-answering tasks, while four summarization tasks add an abstraction dimension. In the terms of terminology from model comprehension research (see Sect. 2.1), the syntactic and semantic questions capture surface-level comprehension, i.e., they are answerable from the presented model content

Table 2. Selected LLMs.

Model	Identifier	Provider	License	Focus	Params
GPT-5.2	gpt-5.2-2025-12-11	OpenAI	Proprietary	Reasoning	n/a
GPT-5 nano	gpt-5-nano-2025-08-07	OpenAI	Proprietary	Reasoning	n/a
Mistral Large 3	mistral-large-2512	Mistral	Open weight	Instruct	675B
Ministral 3	ministral-14b-2512	Mistral	Open weight	Instruct	14B
Llama 4 Scout	Llama-4-Scout-17B-16E	Meta	Open weight	Instruct	109B
Gemma 3	gemma-3-4b-it	Google	Open weight	Instruct	4.3B

alone, whereas the inferential questions and the process-dynamic tasks (trace validation, next-step prediction, anomaly identification) probe the deeper understanding that requires inference beyond the presented content [11]. The seven question-answering tasks are: *Syntactic questions* ask for basic structural elements (nodes, edges). To ensure they are answerable from every format including the textual narrative, they are phrased at a format-independent abstraction level, e.g., asking for activities and decision points rather than BPMN-specific constructs such as gateways. *Semantic questions* test control-flow interpretation, e.g., parallel vs. exclusive branching and loops, or whether two given activities can occur in the same process instance. *Inferential questions* require abstraction from structure to purpose, e.g. inferring the overall business objective from the activity labels. *Trace validation* assesses whether a given activity sequence is executable in the model. *Next-step prediction* asks for identification of the activities reachable from a given state. *Role/responsibility assignment* requests links between activities and the responsible actors. *Deadlock/anomaly identification* expects detection of structural anomalies, e.g., faulty loops. The summarization tasks are: *High-level abstraction* extracts the main purpose of the process without operational detail. *Participant perspective* summarizes the model from the view of a single actor. *Narrative walkthrough* describes the logical flow including actor interactions. *Exception handling* covers alternative paths and conditional logic. For each of the eight processes, we construct one task per type, yielding 88 questions issued to every LLM across all representations.

4.6 Evaluation Pipeline and LLM-as-a-Judge

The responses are collected via a semi-automated Python pipeline iterating over processes, task types, and representation formats. The pipeline assembles the prompts from files and logs the outputs, raw responses, and token counts. Prompting follows a structured zero-shot approach that combines role and contextual prompting. Each prompt places the representation format as the data basis, followed by the task and output format instructions, phrased in English to minimize language bias [13]. To isolate representation effects, the prompt design is held constant across all runs, using format-independent task formulations. The responses are scored using an LLM-as-a-judge, an approach shown to reach high agreement with human judgments [32]. We use single-output scoring against predefined reference answers. The judge (Gemini 3 Flash Preview) receives the Mermaid format as context for context-sensitive judgment. Quality is rated on a discrete four-level scale whose base definitions provide the judge with scoring guardrails: a score of 0 (inadequate) marks responses that are factually wrong, invent elements, or miss the topic entirely, while a score of 1 (weak) indicates that the topic is recognized but essential parts are omitted or the logic is seriously flawed. A score of 2 (acceptable) denotes essentially correct responses with minor inaccuracies, such as mislabeled events, and a score of 3 (perfect) is reserved for precise, complete, and logically sound responses that match the ground truth. For each of the eleven task types, these base definitions are refined into task-specific criteria, which are provided to the judge alongside the base scale. The evaluation is two-dimensional: the score captures answer quality, while the error categories in Table 3 capture the cause of each deviation from the reference answer. The judge was iteratively refined in a proof-of-concept run on a representative subset before the full evaluation. To support reproducibility, the prompt templates, an example process in all representation formats, and the evaluation data are publicly available on Zenodo[1]. Every suboptimal response is assigned at least one error category to capture deviation causes. Complex responses may have multiple categories.

Table 3. Error categories assigned by the judge (main categories).

Category	Summary
Structure and element	Invents non-existent steps or overlooks elements.
Control flow and logic	Confuses decision paths, e.g. parallel versus exclusive, or misreads loops, timers, or termination conditions.
Sequence and routing	Confuses the execution order, ignores dependencies between pools and lanes, or overlooks message flows.
Role and assignment	Attributes tasks to the wrong actors or mixes up responsibilities and system boundaries.
Abstraction and context	Wrong conclusions, inappropriate level of detail, or description of the visual surface instead of the logic.
Generation and technical	Refuses to answer, aborts generation, returns empty output, or gets stuck in repetitive loops.

[1] https://zenodo.org/records/21806811.

5 Results

5.1 Effect of the Representation Format

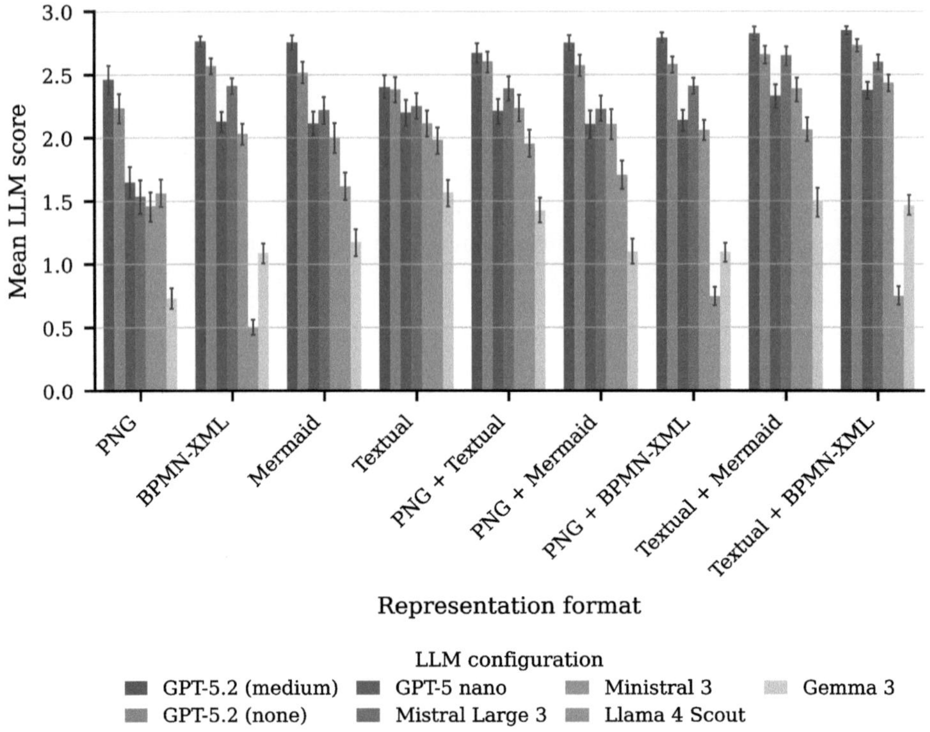

Fig. 2. Mean LLM score per LLM configuration and representation format. Error bars denote 95 % confidence intervals.

Figure 2 shows the mean score per LLM configuration grouped by representation format. Each bar aggregates 264 individual judgments, one for each combination of the eight processes, eleven task types and three iterations. The representation format has a significant influence on the interpretation quality, and this influence varies considerably with the characteristics of the LLM. No single format is best for all LLMs.

Textual Narrative. At first glance, the textual narrative appears weak. For the SOTA LLMs (Mistral Large 3, GPT-5.2), its mean scores rank below those of the structured serializations and the hybrid combinations. However, it is the only isolated format that avoids a collapse for any of the seven LLM configurations, reaching acceptable mean scores (score 2, cf. Sect. 4.6) for all but the smallest LLM, and it is the strongest format for the least capable LLMs.

PNG. The weakest isolated format across all LLMs. It never ranks first and falls clearly behind the serialization and hybrid formats. For smaller LLMs, it fails almost entirely.

Structured Serializations. For the SOTA LLMs, BPMN-XML and Mermaid are the strongest isolated formats. However, their scores are sensitive to the syntactic competence of the LLM. Llama 4 Scout collapses on BPMN-XML, and the mean scores of the configurations span a substantially wider range for the two serializations than for the textual narrative, where even the weakest LLMs stay within one point of the strongest.

Hybrid Formats. Pairing textual narrative with a structured serialization (Textual + Mermaid, Textual + BPMN-XML) consistently achieves the highest scores or matches the strongest isolated format. For SOTA LLMs, combining the textual narrative with the PNG diagram produces a synergy that exceeds isolated formats, though this does not hold for the smaller LLMs. Pairing the PNG diagram with a serialization adds no meaningful value over the serialization alone. Overall, hybrid advantages over isolated serializations are positive but modest and not conclusive across all LLMs.

5.2 Role of LLM Characteristics

Reasoning vs. Instruct. Within the same LLM (GPT-5.2), explicit reasoning yields a stable advantage: reasoning effort medium achieves a cross-format mean of 2.7, while the identical LLM with reasoning effort none scores approximately 0.25 points lower across nearly all formats. The per-format comparison further suggests that interpreting the PNG depends more strongly on reasoning than the textual narrative. Comparing GPT-5.2 (medium) with Mistral Large 3 shows a further gap of approximately 0.25 points. However, as the size and architecture of GPT-5.2 are unknown, this cross-model difference cannot be attributed to reasoning alone.

LLM Size. LLM size correlates with interpretation quality as a general trend, but the relationship is not monotonic. Llama 4 Scout (109B parameters) records a cross-format mean substantially below that of Ministral 3 (14B). This traces back to an LLM-specific deficit with BPMN-XML: Llama 4 Scout scores just above 0.5 on the isolated BPMN-XML, indicating responses that are factually incorrect and miss the core process logic entirely. The same weakness carries into hybrid formats: while the isolated textual narrative reaches almost 2.0, the score for (Textual + BPMN-XML) collapses to approximately 0.65. Gemma 3, the smallest LLM (4.3B), shows the weakest overall results: only the isolated textual narrative yields a mean above 1.5, while all other isolated formats remain at or below approximately 1.0.

5.3 Task Type and Representation Format

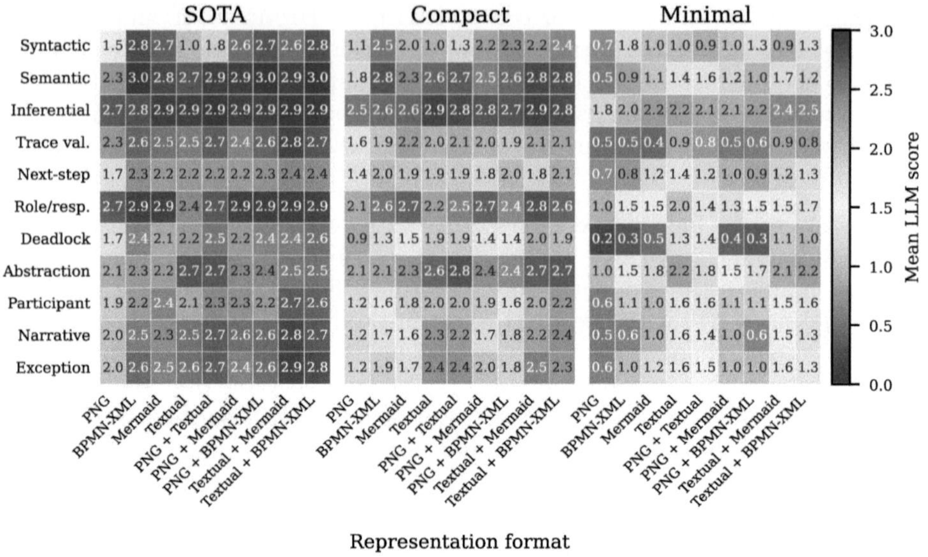

Fig. 3. Mean LLM score per task type and representation format, separated by capability tier.

Figure 3 shows the mean score per task type and representation format, separated into three capability tiers: SOTA (GPT-5.2 in both configurations, Mistral Large 3), compact (GPT-5-nano, Ministral 3), and minimal (Gemma 3). Llama 4 Scout is excluded due to its BPMN-XML anomaly (Sect. 5.2). The tier separation shows which patterns are capability-independent and which are driven by model strength.

Task-Inherent Difficulty. The difficulty ordering of the task types is broadly stable across tiers. Inferential questions yield the highest scores in every tier (SOTA ≥ 2.7, compact ≥ 2.5, minimal ≥ 1.8). They remain the only task on which the minimal tier produces acceptable scores for every format. Process-dynamic tasks that require working through the process model's execution behavior step by step, are the most challenging.

Textual Narrative. The syntactic weakness of the textual narrative is capability-independent. The textual narrative scores 1.0 on syntactic questions in all three tiers. Even the SOTA cannot reliably extract precise structural elements from prose. Its strengths lie at high-level abstraction and inferential questions. For the minimal tier, the textual narrative is the strongest format on most tasks.

PNG. In the compact and minimal tiers, the PNG is the weakest format on nearly every task. In the SOTA tier it trails primarily on syntactic questions, next-step prediction, and deadlock detection. Inferential questions are the consistent exception as they are the best PNG cell in every tier.

Structured Serializations. The serializations dominate syntactic questions in every tier, with BPMN-XML at or above all other formats (2.8, 2.5, and 1.8 in the SOTA, compact, and minimal tier, respectively). Notably, even the smallest LLM reaches its best syntactic score with BPMN-XML, while its performance with the format collapses on most other tasks. In the SOTA and compact tiers, BPMN-XML leads Mermaid on syntactic (2.8 vs. 2.7 and 2.5 vs. 2.0) and semantic questions (3.0 vs. 2.8 and 2.8 vs. 2.3), and both serializations excel at role assignment.

Hybrid Formats. In the SOTA and compact tiers, (Textual + Mermaid) and (Textual + BPMN-XML) achieve near-uniformly strong results, matching or outperforming the isolated formats on most tasks. The exceptions are syntactic questions and high-level abstraction. The largest gains appear for tasks that require precise structural anchors alongside narrative context. In the SOTA tier, participant perspective rises from 2.1 for the textual narrative alone to 2.7 with (Textual + Mermaid). In the minimal tier, the hybrid advantage disappears. The isolated textual narrative matches or outperforms its hybrid combinations on most tasks.

5.4 Error Analysis

Figure 4 shows the number of error instances per error category and representation format, separated by capability tier (Llama 4 Scout excluded). Three observations stand out. First, the representation format strongly affects the number of errors within each tier: (Textual + Mermaid) yields the fewest instances in the SOTA and compact tiers (283 and 451), whereas in the minimal tier the isolated textual narrative produces the fewest (478), consistent with the vanishing hybrid advantage observed in Sect. 5.3. The isolated PNG produces the most errors in the SOTA tier (915), and the BPMN-XML-involving formats the most in the compact and minimal tiers (up to 1,425), mirroring the serialization sensitivity of Sect. 5.2. Second, the error volume scales with capability: normalized by the number of configurations per tier, it approximately doubles with each step down (about 1,850, 3,700, and 7,600 instances per configuration). Third, at least within this experiment, no clear dependency between the format and the error types is recognizable: the ordering of the error categories is preserved across all formats and tiers, with structure and element errors (omissions and hallucinations) dominating, followed by control flow and logic errors, while role and assignment errors are rare and tend to be lowest for BPMN-XML and its hybrids.

6 Discussion

This section interprets the findings, deriving implications for the modeling community and for practice, and discusses the limitations of the study.

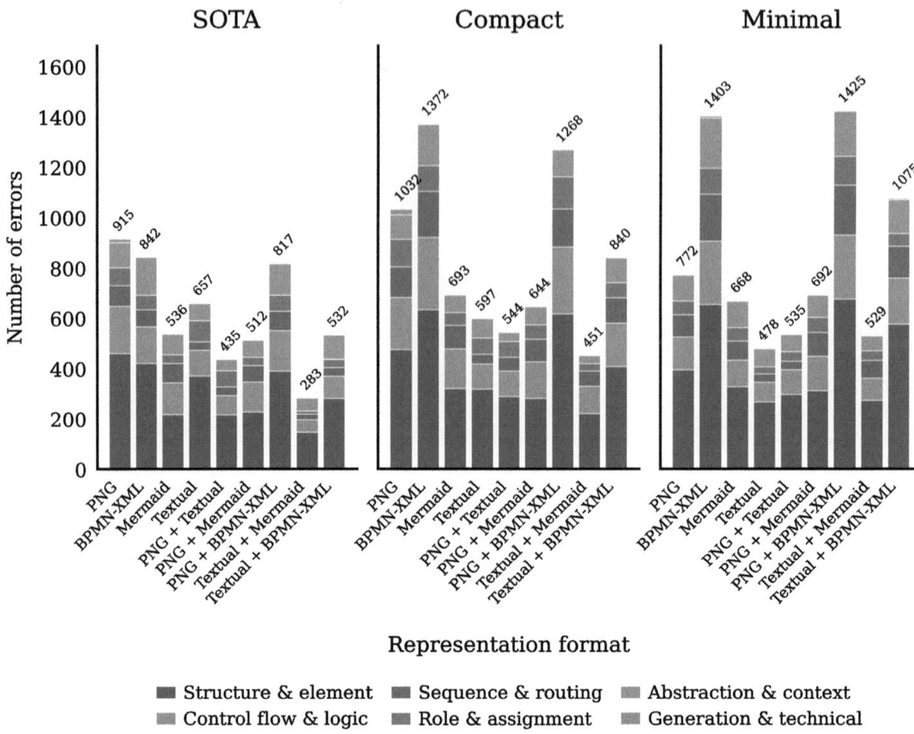

Fig. 4. Distribution of the six main error categories per representation format, separated by capability tier. n is the number of error instances per format.

6.1 Implications for BPM

The central implication is that the representation format is a design variable for LLM-supported BPM tasks. Holding process model content constant, the choice of format can shift interpretation quality substantially, with no single best format across all LLMs tested. Just as factors of visual presentation influence human comprehension of process models, our results establish the representation format as such a factor for LLMs. However, the two do not align: features that support human readability, such as the graphical rendering of control flow, are not necessarily helpful for LLMs. The strongest results come from pairing the textual narrative with a structured serialization, suggesting that LLM interaction treat textual and formal views as complementary.

A second implication concerns the role of the rendered diagram, the primary artifact for human modelers. It is the weakest input for the LLMs tested, which is consistent with [17], who likewise report image inputs underperforming text-based serializations. In behavioral terms, the information graphically encoded in the diagram is not reliably recovered by current mLLMs.

6.2 Implications for Practice

For applying LLMs to BPM tasks, the results yield the following implications. Prompts consisting solely of the rendered diagram proved unreliable in our setup, especially for smaller LLMs, and should be avoided. For small, open-weight LLMs, the textual narrative was the most dependable input. For demanding tasks, the combination of a capable LLM with a hybrid format (textual narrative with a structured serialization) achieved the best results in our setup. The choice of serialization is a trade-off rather than a clear ranking. BPMN-XML scored slightly higher than Mermaid for SOTA and compact tiers on most tasks, but it is considerably more verbose and carried the risk of model-specific failures. Mermaid reached comparable scores at a fraction of the input length and exhibited no such failure mode in our study. Which serialization to choose thus depends on the target LLM and the token budget. The choice between instruct and reasoning configurations involves a similar trade-off. Explicit reasoning improved quality moderately but increases token generation and thereby inference cost and latency.

6.3 Limitations

The limitations of our study concern three levels: the validity of the measurement, the reported format rankings, and the generalizability of the findings.

Measurement Validity. Comprehension is a latent construct that we operationalize as interpretation quality, scored by an LLM-as-a-judge. The scores are therefore themselves LLM outputs and may share systematic biases. We mitigated this by choosing a judge that is not among the evaluated configurations, avoiding the self-preference bias reported in [32], and by calibrating it iteratively on a representative subset. However, a validation against human ratings remains open. Three potential biases still stem from the concrete setup. First, the judge receives the Mermaid format as context, which could favor this format. We confirmed that this bias is marginal with BPMN-XML as judge context, but a more extensive validation across all contexts remains future work. Second, prompt ordering may introduce a recency bias, i.e., the tendency of LLMs to weight content near the end of the prompt more heavily [20]. Third, for heavily flawed responses the judge tends to assign only the dominant error categories. Claims about the error categories should therefore be read at the level of category orderings rather than exact counts. Moreover, cost constraints precluded a stronger judge and repeated judging, so residual judge noise remains.

Format Rankings. Several factors constrain the concrete rankings. Except for the structured serializations, each category is instantiated by a single concrete format - the PNG results, for instance, rest on one rendering style - and the score differences between BPMN-XML and Mermaid show that such single instantiations limit category-level conclusions. Information equivalence across formats rests on deriving all formats from the same BPMN models and phrasing all tasks to be answerable from every format, validated on a sample basis though not exhaustively. Since the PMo dataset is public and activity labels are deliberately non-anonymized, evaluated LLMs may draw on pre-trained domain knowledge, which would primarily inflate absolute scores and task-level profiles. As labels are identical across all formats of a process, the format comparison itself should remain largely unaffected. Disentangling representation-based comprehension from prior knowledge, e.g., through anonymized or counterfactual models, remains future work. Finally, mean aggregation masks LLM-specific profiles and is sensitive to outliers such as Llama 4 Scout. The tier-separated views mitigate but do not remove this, and the observed differences are described behaviorally, without reference to training data or implementation details.

Taken together, these limitations primarily concern absolute scores and the exact format rankings. The central finding - that the representation format substantially affects interpretation quality and thus constitutes a design variable - proved stable across capability tiers, the judge-context check, and both serialization instantiations.

7 Conclusion

This paper investigated how the representation format of a process model affects its interpretation by LLMs. We compared four isolated formats and five hybrid combinations across seven LLM configurations, eight processes, and eleven comprehension tasks, with an LLM-as-a-judge scoring 16,632 responses.

The representation format has a substantial effect on the interpretation quality, and no single format is best for all LLMs. The textual narrative provides the highest floor across LLMs but fails on precise structural questions, while the isolated PNG is the weakest input and fails almost entirely for smaller LLMs. Hybrid combinations of the textual narrative with structured serialization are the strongest formats overall. Within the same LLM, explicit reasoning yields a stable, moderate advantage. LLM size correlates with quality only as a trend: the Llama 4 Scout anomaly on BPMN-XML shows that training matters independently of parameter count. The format strongly affects how many errors occur, whereas no clear dependency between the format and the error types was recognizable in this experiment. Taken together, these findings establish the representation format as a design variable for LLM-supported BPM tasks and yield practice-oriented implications for its selection.

Several directions follow from this work. The control-flow complexity should be scaled, e.g., by linking multiple process models into process landscapes. Since we held the modeling language constant, extending the comparison to other languages like Petri nets would show whether the format effects are BPMN-specific. The knowledge-driven hallucination known from process model generation [16] should be examined for comprehension, ensuring that LLMs interpret the model at hand rather than defaulting to pre-training schemas. Finally, comparing human and LLM comprehension could reveal where the factors diverge.

References

1. Bera, P., Burton-Jones, A., Wand, Y.: Research note–how semantics and pragmatics interact in understanding conceptual models. Inf. Syst. Res. **25**(2), 401–419 (2014)
2. Berti, A., Qafari, M.S.: Leveraging large language models (LLMs) for process mining (technical report) arXiv:2307.12701 (2023)
3. Brissard, A., Cuppens, F., Zouaq, A.: PMo dataset (2025). https://doi.org/10.5281/zenodo.15857589, dataset, Zenodo
4. Brissard, A., Cuppens, F., Zouaq, A.: What is the best process model representation? A comparative analysis for process modeling with large language models. In: Business Process Management (BPM). Springer, Cham (2025)
5. Cardoso, J.: How to measure the control-flow complexity of web processes and workflows. In: Workflow Handbook (2005)
6. Dolha, D.N., Buchmann, R.A.: Generative AI for BPMN process analysis: experiments with multi-modal process representations. In: Perspectives in Business Informatics Research (BIR), pp. 19–35. Springer, Cham (2024)
7. Dumas, M., La Rosa, M., Mendling, J., Reijers, H.A.: Fundamentals of Business Process Management. Springer, Heidelberg (2018)
8. Evermann, J., Wand, Y.: Ontological modeling rules for UML: an empirical assessment. J. Comput. Inf. Syst. **46**(5), 14–29 (2006)
9. Forell, M., Schüler, S.: Modeling meets large language models. In: Modellierung 2024 Satellite Events. Gesellschaft für Informatik e.V. (2024)
10. Franzoi, S., Delwaulle, M., Dyong, J., Schaffner, J., Burger, M., vom Brocke, J.: Using large language models to generate process knowledge from enterprise content. In: Business Process Management (BPM). Springer, Cham (2024)
11. Gemino, A., Wand, Y.: Evaluating modeling techniques based on models of learning. Commun. ACM **46**(10), 79–84 (2003)
12. Grohs, M., Abb, L., Elsayed, N., Rehse, J.R.: Large language models can accomplish business process management tasks. arXiv:2307.09923 (2023)
13. Guo, Y., Conia, S., Zhou, Z., Li, M., Potdar, S., Xiao, H.: Do large language models have an english accent? Evaluating and improving the naturalness of multilingual LLMs. In: Proceedings of 63rd Annual Meeting of the ACL, vol. 1, pp. 3823–3838 (2025)
14. Kamath, U., Keenan, K., Somers, G., Sorenson, S.: Multimodal LLMs. In: Large Language Models: A Deep Dive: Bridging Theory and Practice. Springer, Cham (2024)
15. Kampik, T., et al.: Large process models: a vision for business process management in the age of generative AI. KI - Künstliche Intelligenz **39**(2), 81–95 (2025)
16. Kourani, H., Antonov, A., Berti, A., van der Aalst, W.M.P.: Knowledge-driven hallucination in large language models: an empirical study on process modeling. arXiv:2509.15336 (2025)
17. Kourani, H., et al.: Leveraging large language models for enhanced process model comprehension. Decis. Support Syst. **200**, 114563 (2026)
18. Kourani, H., Berti, A., Schuster, D., van der Aalst, W.M.P.: Process modeling with large language models. arXiv:2403.07541 (2024)
19. Kumar, K., et al.: LLM post-training: a deep dive into reasoning large language models. arXiv:2502.21321 (2025)
20. Liu, N.F., et al.: Lost in the middle: how language models use long contexts. Trans. Assoc. Comput. Linguist. **12**, 157–173 (2024)

21. Mendling, J., Strembeck, M., Recker, J.: Factors of process model comprehension - findings from a series of experiments. Decis. Support Syst. **53**(1), 195–206 (2012)
22. Mili, H., Tremblay, G., Bou Jaoude, G., Lefebvre, É., Elabed, L., El Boussaidi, G.: Business process modeling languages: sorting through the alphabet soup. ACM Comput. Surv. **43**(1), 4:1–4:56 (2010)
23. Mischak, M., Verbruggen, C., Langer, P., Bork, D.: Uncovering LLM's capabilities in model-based question answering for UML class diagrams. In: Enterprise, Business-Process and Information Systems Modeling (BPMDS/EMMSAD), pp. 331–348. Springer, Cham (2026)
24. Möller, M., Winter, M., Reichert, M.: Cognitive factors in process model comprehension - a systematic literature review. Brain Sci. **15**(5) (2025)
25. Object Management Group: Business process model and notation (BPMN), version 2.0.2 (2014)
26. Parsons, J.: An experimental study of the effects of representing property precedence on the comprehension of conceptual schemas. J. Assoc. Inf. Syst. **12**(6) (2011)
27. Parsons, J., Cole, L.: What do the pictures mean? Guidelines for experimental evaluation of representation fidelity in diagrammatical conceptual modeling techniques. Data Knowl. Eng. **55**(3), 327–342 (2005)
28. Rebmann, A., Schmidt, F.D., Glavaš, G., van der Aa, H.: Evaluating the ability of LLMs to solve semantics-aware process mining tasks. In: International Conference on Process Mining (ICPM), pp. 9–16. IEEE (2024)
29. Sveidqvist, K., Mermaid Contributors: Mermaid.js (2026). https://mermaid.js.org/
30. Ye, J., Dash, A., Yin, W., Wang, G.: Beyond end-to-end VLMs: leveraging intermediate text representations for superior flowchart understanding. arXiv:2412.16420 (2024)
31. Zhao, W.X., et al.: A survey of large language models. arXiv:2303.18223 (2023)
32. Zheng, L., et al.: Judging LLM-as-a-judge with MT-Bench and Chatbot Arena. In: Advances in Neural Information Processing Systems, vol. 36, pp. 46595–46623 (2023)

Formalization Matters: Conceptual Modeling with Large Language Models in High, Semi and Low-Formal Tasks

Wolfgang Maass[1], Stephen W. Liddle[2(✉)], and Veda C. Storey[3(✉)]

[1] German Research Center for Artificial Intelligence (DFKI), Saarbrücken, Germany
wolfgang.maass@dfki.de
[2] Brigham Young University, Provo, UT, USA
liddle@byu.edu
[3] Georgia State University, Atlanta, GA, USA
vstorey@gsu.edu

Abstract. Conceptual modeling tasks vary in how explicitly they constrain valid interpretations, from executable schemas to informal stakeholder scenarios. We study how this degree of formalization affects the quality and consistency of LLM outputs, evaluating two open-weight LLMs on three tasks: SQL generation over a relational schema (high-formal), legal clause interpretation (semi-formal), and management decision-making from incident postmortems (low-formal). Comparing outputs against gold standards using recall-based overlap metrics, we find that output quality improves as formalization increases, but variance follows the opposite pattern: high-formal tasks produce higher variance, while low-formal tasks yield lower but more consistently moderate scores. Less formalized tasks are also more susceptible to context drift and normative ambiguity. Formal representations can thus improve LLM-assisted conceptual modeling and reasoning, but require verification mechanisms rather than assumptions of predictable correctness.

Keywords: conceptual modeling · formalization levels · generative AI · large language models · output consistency · variance paradox

1 Introduction

Conceptual modeling remains challenging because it requires understanding and representing the application domain [16,17]. Motivated by the broad versatility of LLMs across domains [4], researchers have begun applying generative AI to automate the creation of initial conceptual models [5,7,9,15,20]. Representations of application domains span a continuum from highly structured, formal representations to loosely structured, informal descriptions [16], although it is not obvious where along this continuum LLM-based automation is reliable.

Generative AI systems perform well on concrete, well-studied tasks such as text summarization, image generation, and code or math benchmarks [14].

P. Fettke et al. (Eds.): ER 2026, LNCS 17125, pp. 57–74, 2027.
https://doi.org/10.1007/978-3-032-40377-3_4

For richer applications, however, they remain prone to hallucination [11], failures of contextual nuance and representational harms [3], and uneven performance across reasoning, factuality, and interaction tasks [2]. The objective of this research is to identify which conceptual modeling tasks LLMs handle well along the structured-to-unstructured continuum.

To carry out our research we build benchmarks for three levels of formalization that capture how structured a domain is. We analyze results for quality and consistency, and discuss the challenges of context drift, variability, and normative ambiguity. We operationalize *formalization* as the degree to which a task's input constraints, solution space, and evaluation criteria are explicitly specified [16,17,21]. SQL generation (formal domain) from a relational schema provides a single correct answer that is verifiable by execution (running a query). Management decisions (low-formal domain) require weighing competing stakeholder interests with no objectively correct solution. Legal interpretations (semi-formal domain) are based on laws but constrained by text and require interpretive reasoning. We note the scope precisely: only the high-formal task operates over an explicit conceptual model (the relational schema); the semi- and low-formal tasks reason over progressively less formal domain representations. Thus the study measures how representation formality affects LLM outputs across tasks relevant to conceptual modeling, rather than how LLMs construct conceptual models *per se*.

Formalization matters for several reasons. LLM training corpora are dominated by unstructured prose, but structured content is deliberately *upsampled*: Llama 3 allocates 17% of tokens to code and 25% to mathematical and reasoning data, despite having a far smaller share of raw web text [8]. This asymmetric exposure may partly explain stronger performance on schema- and code-like tasks (tasks from domains with a high level of formalization). As a task's solution space expands, the model must rely less on pattern matching and more on compositional reasoning, precisely where current LLMs are the weakest [6].

This research makes three main contributions.

1. We describe application domains at high, semi, and low formalization levels: SQL generation, legal clause interpretation, and management decision-making, respectively.
2. We measure output quality and consistency at all three levels using two open-weight models, discovering a variance paradox in which formal tasks produce *higher*, not lower, output variability.
3. We treat formalization as a *continuous* dimension measured at three points rather than a categorical label: we propose a per-instance metric $F(T)$ along three dimensions and show, via a nested-model ablation, that it predicts LLM output quality *beyond* the categorical level encoding.

2 Related Work

Conceptual modeling research supports a progression from informal domain descriptions to explicit, formally constrained conceptual schemas across heterogeneous domains [16]. Wand and Weber's ontological analysis of modeling grammars provides a basis for evaluating the representational adequacy of modeling languages [21], and Olivé treats schemas as logic-based specifications of domain knowledge, constraints, and derivation rules [17]. How formally a domain is described determines what inferences can be validly drawn from a model and the correctness guarantees available to any reasoning agent operating over it. Any reasoning system, logic-based or statistical, should therefore perform better over more formalized representations, because formalization constrains the space of valid interpretations.

A growing body of work applies LLMs to conceptual modeling itself. Cámara et al. [5] assess ChatGPT's ability to produce UML models and report frequent syntactic and semantic defects; Fill et al. [7] survey generative-AI use across modeling notations; and Härer [9] proposes an LLM-based interpreter that generates models in textual syntaxes such as PlantUML. Recent ER-community work continues this line [15, 20]. These efforts share a *generation* framing (prompt an LLM to *produce* a model or model fragment) and evaluate ad hoc, typically on a single notation. What is missing, and what we provide, is a controlled measurement of how the *formalization level of the representation* affects output quality and consistency, holding the task family fixed and using metrics comparable across levels. Rather than proposing another generation method, we characterize where along the formalization spectrum LLM assistance is reliable, and hence when such methods can be trusted.

A key assumption is that LLMs acquire internal representations of the structural regularities of formalized domains, not merely memorized patterns. The strongest evidence comes from mathematics: FunSearch found new solutions to the cap-set problem [19]; AlphaProof, coupling a language model with reinforcement learning over Lean, reached silver-medal level at the 2024 International Mathematical Olympiad [1]; and Knuth [13] reports an LLM-assisted construction for Hamiltonian cycle decompositions he had been unable to find. These successes cluster in highly formalized domains (mathematics, code generation, and formal proof), whereas open-ended tasks such as compositional generalization degrade sharply [6]. We term this asymmetry the *formalization hypothesis*: LLM output quality degrades monotonically as task formalization decreases.

Many benchmarks evaluate LLMs on tasks with well-defined answers, such as competitive-programming problems evaluated by program behavior [14]. Ouyang et al. [18] show that LLM outputs vary across runs even with identical prompts. The relationship between task structure and output variability, however, remains unexplored. We address both gaps by treating formalization as a continuous dimension and measuring quality and variance at three points along it.

3 Method

To explore the effectiveness of using LLMs for modeling, we apply multiple open-weight models to modeling tasks at different levels of formalization and measure the results against benchmarks. Three hypotheses test the effectiveness:

H1: Quality gradient. *LLM output quality decreases as domain formalization decreases.* Models trained on corpora of structured content should produce higher-quality outputs when the solution space is tightly constrained.

H2: Variance gradient. *Output variance across repeated runs increases as domain formalization decreases.* Less-constrained tasks have more degrees of freedom, so successive runs should diverge more.

H3: Length–quality mediation. *Greater response length corresponds to higher recall scores regardless of formalization level.* Longer outputs raise the probability of coincidentally matching gold-standard terms; controlling for length should therefore narrow apparent quality differences between models.

3.1 Experiments

To test H1–H3 we require tasks that differ systematically in how closely their inputs constrain acceptable outputs, while holding constant whether tasks are self-contained, have gold standards, and span graded levels of complexity.[1] We selected one domain task for each level of formalization as follows:

High-Formal: SQL Generation. Generate the correct SQL query given a relational schema derived from a conceptual model of a sales/order database and a natural-language question. The schema generated from the conceptual model has precise syntax and semantics; correctness is verifiable by execution. This consisted of 100 tasks over the Northwind schema, spanning simple joins to complex multi-table queries with aggregations and subqueries.

Semi-formal: Legal Clause Interpretation. For a given legal scenario, determine whether an action is permitted, required, or prohibited under a contractual clause. The clause text constrains the answer but requires interpretive reasoning about the scope and exceptions. This consisted of 59 tasks across 11 clause categories (assignment, termination, liability, etc.) drawn from the Contract Understanding Atticus Dataset (CUAD) [10]. The conceptual model is semi-formal, with well-defined categories corresponding to entities and natural-language descriptions of relationships and constraints.

Low-Formal: Management Decision-Making. Given a postmortem description of a software incident, recommend a management response when there are multiple stakeholders. No single correct answer exists; quality is assessed by coverage of relevant considerations. This dataset has 31 tasks across 9 incident categories derived from publicly documented reports (e.g., GitHub's 2018 split-brain outage; Knight Capital's 2012 trading loss). Gold standards enumerate key considerations without prescribing a unique solution. The conceptual model is low-formal, being represented mostly in natural language (except for the list of stakeholders).

Table 1 summarizes the input structure and expected output; full prompt templates are available in the reproducibility repository. All tasks adhere to

[1] Reproducibility: https://anonymous.4open.science/r/er26-16F0/.

three principles ensuring valid cross-level comparison: (i) self-contained inputs: the input is a sufficient statistic for the correct output, so the model need not condition on any context beyond the prompt; (ii) gold standards for every task[2]; and (iii) graded complexity, with tasks within each level spanning a complexity range (e.g., simple vs. complex queries; moderate vs. complex management scenarios).

Table 1. Task structure by formalization level.

Level	Input Structure	Expected Output
High-formal	`schema` (Northwind DDL, shared across all 100 tasks), `question` (natural-language query)	Raw SQL query (no markdown, no explanation)
Semi-formal	`clause_text` (verbatim contract clause from CUAD), `scenario` (factual situation), `question` (legal interpretation question)	Legal interpretation citing specific clause terms
Low-formal	`scenario` (postmortem incident), `stakeholders` (named roles), `question` (management decision question)	Multi-perspective analysis addressing stakeholder interests and tradeoffs

To empirically test our hypotheses, we combine the three formalization levels into a continuous *formalization metric* $F(T)$ along three dimensions. *Output-space cardinality* $C(T)$ is the number of distinct outputs judged correct: small for SQL (one canonical query plus syntactic variants), bounded for legal interpretation, and effectively unbounded for management decisions. *Syntactic constraint density* $S(T)$ is the proportion of the output determined by grammar rules of the target language rather than by model choice (high for SQL, loose rhetorical conventions for legal, none beyond natural language for management). *Evaluation decidability* $D(T)$ captures whether correctness can be determined algorithmically (D=1, SQL execution), by bounded expert judgment (D=0.5, legal clause matching), or only by open-ended assessment (D=0, management quality).

We define $F(T) = \frac{1}{3}(\hat{C}(T) + S(T) + D(T))$, where $\hat{C}(T) = 1/\log_2(1 + C(T))$ normalizes cardinality to $[0, 1]$ (the +1 offset maps the unique-answer case C=1 to $\hat{C}$=1). This ensures diminishing returns: moving from one to two defensible answers reduces formalization more than moving from one to two hundred.

[2] High-formal gold standards are reference SQL queries generated with ChatGPT 5.1 (OpenAI) tool assistance but fully tested, evaluated, and revised by a human expert. Low-formal gold standards, and 57 of the 59 semi-formal gold standards, were generated by Claude Sonnet 4.6 (Anthropic) using structured annotation prompts that enforce self-containment and traceability to the input text; the remaining two semi-formal items were generated by Claude Opus 4.6. Neither ChatGPT nor Claude is a model under evaluation. Expert validation is in progress; annotation spreadsheets and the scoring protocol are available.

Crucially, $F(T)$ is computed *per task instance*, not merely per level. For each of the 190 tasks, $C(T)$, $S(T)$, and $D(T)$ are derived programmatically from task metadata and gold-output structural features (e.g., $S(T)$ from SQL-keyword and punctuation density on the gold query for high-formal tasks, and from analogous markers for the other levels), yielding a continuous F value that varies *within* each level as well as across levels. Table 2 reports the per-dimension values, and Sect. 4.6 tests whether this instance-level $F(T)$ carries explanatory power beyond the categorical high/semi/low encoding.

Table 2. Formalization metric $F(T)$ by level: per-dimension inputs and resulting F (mean ± std over task instances). $\hat{C}$ is normalized output-space cardinality, S syntactic constraint density, D evaluation decidability. F varies within levels because $C(T)$ and $S(T)$ are computed per instance.

Level	n	$\hat{C}$	S (mean)	D	$F(T)$
High	100	0.558	0.880	1.0	0.813 ± 0.078
Semi	59	0.273	0.423	0.5	0.399 ± 0.029
Low	31	0.141	0.255	0.0	0.132 ± 0.008

In this study, we use two open-weight instruction-tuned models: Mistral-7B-Instruct-v0.3 [12] and Llama-3.1-8B-Instruct [8]. All inference runs locally with no external API calls on NVIDIA GPUs (A100-SXM4-80GB or RTX PRO 6000 Blackwell) in an HPC cluster at Saarland Univ., through a unified wrapper that loads each model with 4-bit NF4 quantization, applies its chat template, and strips the input prompt from the generated output.

To assess output consistency, each task is executed $K=5$ times with identical prompts and temperature ($T=0.7$). Generation is capped at 256 new tokens at the high-formal level and 512 at the semi- and low-formal levels, reflecting the differing output lengths the three response formats require. Results are stored in JSONL with a `run_index` field (0–4) for consistency analysis.

Because these caps bind on the longer-form conditions, we verified that they do not produce the variance result reported in Sect. 4.1. Truncation is essentially absent for Mistral at the high- and semi-formal levels (5% and 2% of outputs), yet its within-task variance of word overlap still falls by a factor of 2.6 across that transition (.0042 → .0016). Conversely, Llama's truncation rate is nearly constant across all three levels (90%, 92%, 94%) while its within-task variance falls by an order of magnitude (.0059 → .0005). A near-uniform censoring rate cannot generate a monotone gradient, so the ordering reported in Table 6 is not an artifact of the token budget. Table 3 summarizes the experimental data.

3.2 Evaluation

To evaluate our experimental results, we used quality and consistency metrics, applying appropriate statistical tests to assess significance. We also developed a rubric for human expert evaluation to cross-check the automated metrics.

Table 3. Dataset summary across formalization levels and models.

Level	Model	Tasks	K	Records	Avg. Resp. Len.
High-formal	Llama-3.1-8B	100	5	500	967
High-formal	Mistral-7B	100	5	500	212
Semi-formal	Llama-3.1-8B	59	5	295	2357
Semi-formal	Mistral-7B	59	5	295	833
Low-formal	Llama-3.1-8B	31	5	155	2908
Low-formal	Mistral-7B	31	5	155	2557
Total		190		1900	

Quality Metrics. A challenge is finding metrics applicable uniformly across all three levels. Domain-specific metrics (execution correctness for SQL, inter-annotator agreement for legal) cannot be compared across levels. We therefore adopt text-overlap metrics against expert gold standards as the *cross-level* metric: while coarser than domain-specific alternatives, this ensures that observed differences reflect the formalization gradient rather than incompatibilities among metrics. For the high-formal level we *additionally* report a rigorous domain-specific metric, SQL execution accuracy (Sect. 4.3), to verify that the overlap-based ranking is not an artifact of the proxy; the two agree. We use three recall-oriented overlap measures against the gold standard, where W denotes the set of unique lower-cased words: W_{gold} for words from the gold standard and W_{pred} for words from the LLM prediction (i.e., output):

- *Word overlap*: $|W_{\text{pred}} \cap W_{\text{gold}}|/|W_{\text{gold}}|$, capturing broad topical coverage.
- *Bigram overlap*: same ratio over word bigrams, sensitive to phrasal structure (e.g., `GROUP BY` vs. separate `GROUP` and `BY`; "material breach" vs. unrelated occurrences of either word).
- *Key-term recall*: fraction of distinctive gold-standard words (length > 3, excluding stopwords) present in the prediction, focusing on domain-specific content words (table names, legal terms, stakeholder labels).

All three focus on recall. They measure how much of the gold standard is recovered, not how much of the prediction is relevant. This is deliberate but introduces a known bias toward verbose responses (see H3 and Sect. 5.4). Alongside recall we therefore also report precision, $|W_{\text{pred}} \cap W_{\text{gold}}|/|W_{\text{pred}}|$, and the harmonic-mean F_1, which penalize irrelevant content. Table 4 summarizes these metrics by formalization level and model.

Consistency Metrics ($K=5$). We measure *unique outputs*, the number of distinct responses across K runs per task after lowercasing and whitespace normalization (K = complete inconsistency; 1 = perfect reproducibility); and *perfect consistency*, the percentage of tasks producing identical output across all K runs (the strictest reliability criterion).

Table 4. Quality metrics against gold standards by formalization level and model, all computed on a single raw-text word-set representation (letters only, length ≥ 3; key-terms length > 4 minus stopwords). Pred/Gold is the mean character-length ratio. Llama's recall lead at the high-formal level reverses under precision and F_1: its longer outputs recover more gold terms but at much lower precision.

Level	Model	Word			Key-term			Pred/Gold
		Rec.	Prec.	F_1	Rec.	Prec.	F_1	
High	Llama	.800	.547	.615	.791	.555	.620	7.00×
High	Mistral	.764	.823	**.777**	.748	.813	**.763**	1.06×
Semi	Llama	.251	.212	.225	.181	.153	.162	1.73×
Semi	Mistral	.181	.273	.215	.124	.195	.149	0.61×
Low	Llama	.231	.398	.291	.204	.352	.257	0.64×
Low	Mistral	.229	.396	.290	.205	.353	.259	0.57×

Statistical Tests. Shapiro-Wilk tests reject normality for all quality distributions, so we adopt a non-parametric pipeline operating on ranks. A Kruskal-Wallis H test (omnibus test of H1) checks whether central tendencies differ across the three levels. Mann-Whitney U tests with Bonferroni correction ($k = 3$) localize pairwise effects, with high → semi and semi → low as the theoretically motivated transitions. Levene's test, which is relatively robust to departures from normality, addresses H2 by testing equality of spreads. And rank-biserial correlation $r \in [-1, +1]$ quantifies effect size so that statistical significance is distinguished from practical magnitude.

Human Evaluation Protocol. Because automated overlap metrics are proxies for semantic quality, we designed an expert rubric applicable across all levels:

3 (Excellent): Correct and complete: SQL executes and returns the right result set; legal identifies all applicable provisions and reaches the correct conclusion; management covers all key stakeholders and tradeoffs.
2 (Adequate): Substantially correct; captures the core answer but misses secondary considerations.
1 (Partial): Some relevant content but missing major elements or containing significant errors.
0 (Incorrect): Wrong, irrelevant, or non-responsive.

Each output is scored independently by two annotators; inter-annotator agreement is measured by Cohen's kappa (target $\kappa \geq 0.70$). A stratified sample of 30 outputs (10 per level, balanced across models and complexity tags) is scored in a pilot round to calibrate the rubric before full annotation. Expert evaluation has begun through qualitative inspection of sampled outputs, but comprehensive rubric-based annotation is not yet fully complete.

4 Results

4.1 Quality and Variance Metrics (H1 and H2)

To assess H1, we apply statistical tests and perform pairwise comparisons between the metrics described in Table 4, which shows that quality drops sharply with decreasing formalization. Averaging across models, word overlap falls from .782 (high) to .216 (semi) and .230 (low); the dominant gradient is the high-to-semi drop, after which semi- and low-formal tasks occupy a similar quality band (the small semi–low differences are examined in Sect. 5.2). Kruskal-Wallis tests confirm that the across-level gradient is highly significant for all three metrics (word overlap $H = 1410.3$; bigram overlap $H = 1313.2$; key-term recall $H = 1450.5$; all $p < 10^{-285}$). All overlap and length metrics use a single raw-text representation (Table 4).

Mann-Whitney U tests with Bonferroni correction reveal that the dominant quality drop occurs between high-formal and semi-formal levels. (See Table 5.) The semi → low transition reveals smaller, metric-dependent differences.

Table 5. Pairwise Mann-Whitney U tests for the adjacent transitions (Bonferroni-corrected, $k = 3$). Effect size r is rank-biserial correlation. The high → low comparison (omitted) is significant at the same level as high → semi for every metric ($|r| \geq .971$, $p_{\text{corr}} < 10^{-146}$).

Metric	Comparison	Δ	p_{corr}	r	Sig.
Word↑	High → Semi	+.566	1.9×10^{-238}	−.989	***
	Semi → Low	−.014	8.0×10^{-14}	+.308	***
Bigram↑	High → Semi	+.419	1.1×10^{-217}	−.945	***
	Semi → Low	+.005	4.3×10^{-24}	+.415	***
KeyTerm↑	High → Semi	+.618	1.0×10^{-240}	−.994	***
	Semi → Low	−.052	3.1×10^{-43}	+.562	***

Significance codes: *** $p < 0.001$.

To assess H2, we use Levene's test (median-centered), which yields a striking finding: output variance *decreases* monotonically with decreasing formalization. For word overlap, per-level variance falls from .0226 (high) to .0115 (semi) to .0008 (low) ($W = 186.4$, $p = 1.2 \times 10^{-74}$); bigram overlap (.0548/.0054/.0002; $W = 551.4$) and key-term recall (.0240/.0118/.0009; $W = 214.0$) follow the same high $\gg$ semi $\gg$ low gradient (both $p < 10^{-83}$). The IQR (interquartile range) follows the same pattern: .198/.110/.041 (word overlap) from high to low. This suggests that high-formal tasks produce a bimodal distribution (either close to the gold-standard SQL or completely wrong), while low-formal tasks consistently cover similar conceptual ground even when wording differs.

Separating Across-Run from Across-Task Variance. H2 concerns variance *across repeated runs*, but the pooled per-record variance tested above mixes two distinct quantities: run-to-run variation within a task and differences between tasks within a level. Table 6 decomposes them: for each task we compute the variance of word overlap across its $K = 5$ runs (within-task), and separately the variance of per-task means (between-task). The between-task component dominates (at the high-formal level, .0187 of the .0226 pooled variance), so the Levene test above primarily reflects task heterogeneity. Critically, the within-task, across-run variance (the quantity H2 actually names) shows the *same* monotonic decrease with formalization (.0050 → .0017 → .0005; Kruskal-Wallis $H = 51.1$, $p = 7.9 \times 10^{-12}$). The refutation of H2 is thus robust: however variance is measured, it decreases as formalization decreases.

Table 6. Variance decomposition of word overlap by level (pooled over models). *Within-task* is the mean over tasks of the variance across the $K = 5$ runs of a task (the quantity H2 names); *between-task* is the variance of per-task means; *pooled* is the variance over all run-level records (the quantity tested by Levene's statistic). All three components decrease monotonically with formalization.

Level	#Tasks	Within-task	Between-task	Pooled
High	100	.00502	.01866	.02260
Semi	59	.00174	.01013	.01145
Low	31	.00045	.00045	.00080

Kruskal-Wallis on within-task variance across levels: $H = 51.1$, $p = 7.9 \times 10^{-12}$.

4.2 Consistency and Length (H3)

Neither Llama nor Mistral achieves meaningful consistency across runs. Averaging across levels, nearly every task produces K unique outputs across $K = 5$ runs (average unique outputs ≈ 5.0 for all conditions except Mistral on high-formal SQL, where the average is 3.8). The only exception is Mistral-7B on high-formal SQL, where 7 out of 100 tasks (7%) produce identical outputs across all runs. Perfect consistency is 0% for all other level/model combinations.

On the recall-oriented metrics, Llama-3.1-8B scores higher than Mistral-7B at the high- and semi-formal levels (Mann-Whitney U, Bonferroni-corrected $p < 10^{-3}$), and the two models converge at the low-formal level ($p > 0.99$). This recall advantage, however, is an artifact of verbosity, and it reverses under precision (Table 4). Because the recall metrics divide by $|W_{\text{gold}}|$ and do not penalize irrelevant prediction content, Llama's much longer outputs (high-formal: 7.0× gold length vs. Mistral's 1.1×) inflate its recall. Precision and F_1 tell the opposite story at the high-formal level, where Mistral's concise queries achieve far higher precision (.823 vs. .547 word precision) and F_1 (.777 vs. .615). Under F_1, then, Mistral is the stronger high-formal model, not Llama. At the semi-formal level the models are near-tied under F_1 (.225 vs. .215), and at the low-formal level they remain statistically indistinguishable on every measure.

These results confirm H3 (length–quality mediation): longer responses raise recall-oriented scores without a corresponding gain in precision. The inter-model recall gap is largest where the length difference is largest (high-formal) and vanishes where both models produce comparably short outputs (low-formal, 0.6× gold length for both). Under precision, which penalizes irrelevant content, the advantage of verbosity disappears (and at the high-formal level reverses), so Llama's recall lead reflects length-inflated lexical overlap, rather than superior understanding.

4.3 High-Formal Execution Accuracy

Overlap metrics are coarsest precisely where correctness is objective. We therefore complement the overlap scores with execution accuracy. We load the Northwind schema and data into an in-process analytical database (DuckDB) and execute both the gold and the predicted SQL, scoring a prediction correct when its result set exactly matches the gold's (order-insensitive unless the query specifies `ORDER BY`; the Spider-style execution-accuracy criterion). Five of the 100 gold queries use constructs outside the engine's dialect and are excluded, leaving 95 gradeable tasks ($\times K=5$). Table 7 reports the results.

Table 7. High-formal SQL execution accuracy (exact result-set match against a populated Northwind database, Spider-style). *runs* is the fraction of predictions that execute without error; *exact* is computed over the 95 gradeable tasks whose gold query executes in the engine.

Model	Metric	Easy	Medium	Hard	Overall
Mistral	runs	97%	63%	31%	62%
	exact	68%	53%	22%	**49%**
Llama	runs	94%	72%	55%	72%
	exact	67%	62%	52%	**61%**

Execution accuracy corroborates the overlap-based analysis on an objective metric. Llama outperforms Mistral (61% vs. 49% exact), the same direction as the recall and F_1 comparisons, confirming that the model ranking is not an artifact of the overlap proxy. Two points stand out. First, accuracy is far from perfect even at the formal level: fewer than two-thirds of queries return the correct result, and 19–25% of queries that *execute* still return a wrong result set, reinforcing that formalization raises the ceiling but does not guarantee correctness, so verification remains necessary. Second, accuracy declines monotonically with query difficulty (easy > medium > hard for both models), an execution-grounded instance of the within-domain gradient examined next.

4.4 Robustness and Validity Checks

A potential confound in the cross-level comparison is that the three formalization levels use different task domains (databases, law, management), so observed quality differences might reflect domain difficulty rather than formalization *per se*. To address this, we exploit the complexity tags embedded in our task sets to test whether the formalization gradient operates *within* a single domain.

High-Formal (SQL). The 100 SQL tasks are tagged by difficulty: 20 easy, 55 medium, and 25 hard tasks. These difficulty levels represent a within-domain formalization gradient: easy queries have a more constrained output space ($C(T)$ closer to 1) than hard multi-table queries where multiple valid join strategies exist. Comparing word overlap across difficulty tags, we observe a decline from .831 (easy) to .798 (medium) to .708 (hard), mirroring the cross-level pattern within a single domain. Execution accuracy shows the same monotonic within-domain gradient (Table 7: Mistral 68% → 53% → 22%; Llama 67% → 62% → 52%), so the gradient is not an artifact of the overlap metric.

Low-Formal (Management). The 31 management tasks span 9 incident categories with two complexity levels (moderate and complex). Complex scenarios, which involve more stakeholders and competing objectives, yield lower gold-standard overlap (.223 vs. .240 for moderate), consistent with the prediction that expanding the solution space reduces overlap-based quality.

These within-domain results strengthen the claim that formalization, not domain, drives the quality gradient; the effect size is smaller within than across domains, as expected, since the within-domain formalization range is narrower.

A further threat to construct validity arises when gold standards are generated by the same model family under evaluation, because overlap metrics may then reward shared stylistic tendencies rather than genuine task understanding. Here that risk is low: high-formal gold standards are human-curated, execution-tested reference queries, and semi- and low-formal gold standards were generated by Claude models, which are architecturally and organizationally independent of both evaluated models, using annotation prompts that enforce traceability to the input text. Neither evaluated model could therefore benefit from stylistic overlap with its own prior outputs in the gold standard.

4.5 Robustness to Sampling Temperature

Because the variance paradox could be an artifact of the default sampling temperature ($T = 0.7$), we re-ran the full benchmark (all three levels, both models) at $T \in \{0, 0.3, 0.7, 1.0\}$ ($K = 1$ for greedy $T = 0$, $K = 5$ otherwise). Table 8 reports per-level within-task (across-run) variance of word overlap at each temperature. The paradoxical ordering (*more* formal tasks show *higher* run-to-run variance) holds at every sampled temperature for both models. As expected, absolute variance grows with temperature (and is zero at $T = 0$, where greedy decoding is deterministic), but the high > semi > low ordering is invariant. The quality gradient is likewise stable: the dominant high → semi drop persists at all temperatures (high word overlap .76–.80 vs. semi .18–.25), with mean quality varying by less than .03 across the temperature range. The paper's two central findings are therefore not sampling-regime artifacts.

Table 8. Within-task (across-run) variance of word overlap by level and temperature (Mistral/Llama). The variance paradox (high > semi > low) holds at every $T > 0$ for both models; $T = 0$ is deterministic so variance is zero by construction.

T	Var_{High} (M/L)	Var_{Semi} (M/L)	Var_{Low} (M/L)
0.0	.0000/.0000	.0000/.0000	.0000/.0000
0.3	.0021/.0035	.0010/.0023	.0004/.0005
0.7	.0039/.0068	.0014/.0020	.0005/.0006
1.0	.0051/.0071	.0015/.0031	.0005/.0004

4.6 Validating the Formalization Metric $F(T)$

A natural objection is that $F(T)$ merely relabels the three levels, adding no information beyond the categorical high/semi/low encoding. Because $F(T)$ is computed per task instance (Sect. 3), we test this with a nested-model ablation over all 190 tasks, regressing per-task mean quality (word overlap) on: M1, the categorical level alone; M2, $F(T)$ alone; and M3, level $+ F(T)$. If $F(T)$ carried no information beyond the level labels, M3 would not improve on M1.

It does. M3 significantly improves fit over M1 (nested $F_{1,186} = 9.31$, $p = 2.6 \times 10^{-3}$; $\Delta\text{AIC} = -7.3$), with a positive within-model coefficient on $F(T)$ ($\beta_F = 0.408 \pm 0.134$, $t = 3.05$). Adding a per-level F slope (M4) does not further improve fit ($p = 0.77$), so a single global slope suffices. The instance-level $F(T)$ therefore predicts output quality *beyond* the level to which a task belongs. In contrast, $F(T)$ does *not* predict per-task quality *variance* beyond the level encoding ($p = 0.65$), consistent with the refutation of H2: variance is governed by level-scale bimodality rather than by fine-grained formalization.

Within-level Pearson correlations between $F(T)$ and mean quality are positive at all three levels (high $r = 0.22$, $p = 0.03$; semi $r = 0.23$, $p = 0.08$; low $r = 0.42$, $p = 0.02$), showing that the signal is not purely a between-level artifact. We further guard against a concern that both $F(T)$ (through gold-based $S(T)$) and word overlap (through $|W_{\text{gold}}|$) depend on gold-text features, by taking out the gold token count and keyword fraction. The within-level signal is robust at the low-formal level (partial $R^2 = 0.14$; coefficient inflation 2.2%) but is substantially attenuated at the high- and semi-formal levels (inflation 168% and 78%; partial $R^2 \leq 0.03$). Accordingly, we treat the *cross-level* ablation (M3 vs. M1) as the primary evidence that $F(T)$ adds information beyond the categorical encoding, and report the within-level correlations with this caveat.

5 Discussion

This research has investigated performance of LLMs in conceptual modeling activities by applying them to modeling applications at three levels of formalization: generating SQL queries over a relational schema derived from a conceptual model (high), interpreting semi-formal CUAD clause categories and constraints (semi), and identifying actors, goals, tradeoffs, and recommendations from stakeholder/incident decision descriptions (low). The results show that the differences in the formalization level of a modeling application are not simply a matter of convenience. Rather, formalization can serve as a predictor of both LLM output quality and variability. The formalization metric $F(T)$ provides a way to quantify where a task appears on the formalization gradient spectrum and, consequently, what output quality to expect from LLM-based creation or analysis of a model.

5.1 Findings

Of the three hypotheses derived from the formalization hypothesis and related work, two are supported (H1: quality gradient; H3: length–quality mediation) and one is refuted (H2: variance gradient).

H1 was supported: quality declined sharply as formalization decreased. Because the same pattern appeared both across domains and within domains of differing complexity (Sects. 4.1 and 4.4), formalization is associated with LLM reasoning quality beyond domain alone, extending the conceptual modeling intuition that semantic precision improves automated reasoning.

The refutation of H2 is the most consequential finding: output variance *decreases* rather than increases with decreasing formalization. Formalization therefore raises expected quality while widening the variance distribution, implying that schema-driven LLM applications should not assume stable correctness. Our data establish the need for verification (the bimodal outcome distribution and the 49–61% execution accuracy) but do not by themselves establish that a particular mitigation is sufficient; verification against ground truth and, as a design heuristic warranting further study, retry-and-select strategies are therefore advisable rather than proven remedies.

H3 was supported in its mechanism (Sect. 4.2): response length inflates recall-oriented scores without a corresponding gain in precision, so the verbosity premium reflects lexical overlap inflation rather than superior understanding, exactly as H3 predicts.

5.2 Pairwise Comparison Anomaly and Consistency

The pairwise results (Table 5) reveal a nuanced pattern. The semi → low transition is small in magnitude but, because of the large sample, statistically significant, and for word and key-term overlap it is a mild *reversal*: low-formal tasks score slightly *higher* than semi-formal. This likely reflects vocabulary rather than reasoning: legal gold standards use specialized terminology, whereas management gold standards use general analytical vocabulary that models match more easily. Evaluation instruments independent of domain vocabulary, such as expert assessment and within-domain analysis, are therefore needed.

The near-total absence of run-to-run consistency, even on objectively correct SQL tasks, highlights a fundamental challenge. At $T = 0.7$ (a typical general-purpose temperature setting), both models generate semantically similar but lexically distinct outputs on every run; the 7% perfect consistency achieved by Mistral on SQL (vs. 0% for Llama) may reflect Mistral's more concise output style, which leaves less room for lexical variation.

5.3 Implications for Modeling

High-formal tasks grounded in a conceptual model that led to a precise relational schema yield the highest quality, supporting LLM use for schema-driven code generation, query synthesis, and model transformation. Semi-formal tasks (legal clause interpretation) show a substantial quality decline (word overlap drops by over 70% relative to high-formal), indicating that LLM-assisted reasoning over semi-formal notations (UML constraints, business rules, structured requirements) is feasible, but requires careful verification. The quality plateau between semi-formal and low-formal levels suggests that the most important reliability boundary for LLM-based automation lies at the high $\rightarrow$ semi transition, not the semi $\rightarrow$ low transition.

The quality gradient provides an empirical rationale for the long-standing conceptual modeling prescription to formalize where possible: investing in more formal representations (e.g., structured schemas, constraint languages for business rules) is effective when LLMs are used as reasoning engines. Combined with the variance paradox, the implication is that formal representations both raise expected quality and make verification *necessary*, not merely desirable.

We use *context drift* to denote the tendency of generated outputs to diverge from the concepts, constraints, stakeholder relationships, or assumptions grounded in the input text. In qualitative inspection of sampled LLM outputs, we observed that context drift was minimal in the high-formal SQL tasks because the conceptual schema and executable semantics tightly constrained the solution space. In the semi-formal and low-formal tasks, drift occurred when LLMs generalized beyond the input text or introduced unsupported interpretations.

We use *normative ambiguity* to denote situations in which multiple outputs are defensible because evaluation depends on competing stakeholder values, organizational priorities, or socially contingent judgments rather than formally decidable correctness criteria. Normative ambiguity is largely absent in the SQL tasks, bounded in the legal tasks by contractual language and precedent, and most pronounced in the management tasks where tradeoffs among stakeholders often lack a single objectively correct resolution.

These observations help explain the formalization gradient. As formalization decreases, the conceptual boundaries constraining interpretation weaken, increasing susceptibility to context drift and normative ambiguity even when outputs remain superficially coherent.

5.4 Limitations

The main results rely on text-overlap metrics to approximate semantic quality. The primary metrics are recall-oriented and thus biased toward verbose outputs; we mitigate this by also reporting precision and F_1 (Table 4), though any overlap metric remains a coarse proxy for correctness. Expert annotation under the unified 0–3 rubric will provide the finer-grained human judgment that overlap metrics cannot, but it is not yet complete, so the findings currently lack independent human validation.

Both evaluated models are 7–8B parameters. Generalization of the findings to 70B+ models, where better instruction following and richer internal representations could alter the formalization gradient, is not warranted. The variance paradox is, however, robust to sampling temperature: a full sweep over $T \in \{0, 0.3, 0.7, 1.0\}$ (Sect. 4.5) reproduces the within-task variance ordering (high > semi > low) at every sampled temperature for both models, and the dominant high → semi quality drop persists throughout. Semi-formal and low-formal gold standards were generated by Claude models rather than by domain experts, although expert validation is in progress. Thus, the corresponding overlap metrics should be considered as being in agreement with an LLM reference, rather than as absolute correctness. Finally, the study is observational and cannot determine whether formalization *causes* the observed quality differences or whether task properties (domain, length, complexity) drive the gradient.

6 Conclusion and Future Work

We investigated how task formalization affects LLM performance in conceptual modeling applications. Across high-formal SQL generation, semi-formal legal clause interpretation, and low-formal management decision-making, output quality improved as formalization increased while output variance followed the opposite pattern, and less formalized tasks were more susceptible to context drift and normative ambiguity. Formal representations can therefore improve LLM-assisted reasoning, but because formalization does not make outputs more predictable, verification mechanisms must accompany them.

Several extensions follow directly. The dominant quality drop occurs at the high → semi boundary, and both word and key-term recall show a mild reversal at the semi → low transition; whether this reflects genuine non-monotonicity or an artifact of domain vocabulary warrants investigation with richer instruments, including the expert 0–3 rubric and within-domain complexity analysis. We have also prepared an obituary dataset of 100 obituaries (two per US state, with annotated person/relation extractions corresponding to a conceptual model) as a semi-structured complement to the SQL benchmark; this dataset will join future experiments alongside additional datasets and larger models.[3]

[3] Both the SQL and obituary datasets are available upon request.

References

1. AlphaProof Team, AlphaGeometry Team: AI achieves silver-medal standard solving International Mathematical Olympiad problems. Google DeepMind Blog (2024). https://deepmind.google/discover/blog/ai-solves-imo-problems-at-silver-medal-level/
2. Bang, Y., Cahyawijaya, S., Lee, N., et al.: A multitask, multilingual, multimodal evaluation of ChatGPT on reasoning, hallucination, and interactivity. In: Proceedings of the 13th International Joint Conference on Natural Language Processing and the 3rd Conference of the Asia-Pacific Chapter of the Association for Computational Linguistics (IJCNLP-AACL) (2023). https://arxiv.org/abs/2302.04023
3. Bender, E.M., Gebru, T., McMillan-Major, A., Shmitchell, S.: On the dangers of stochastic parrots: can language models be too big? In: Proceedings of the 2021 ACM Conference on Fairness, Accountability, and Transparency (FAccT), pp. 610–623 (2021). https://doi.org/10.1145/3442188.3445922
4. Brown, T.B., Mann, B., Ryder, N.: Language models are few-shot learners. In: Advances in Neural Information Processing Systems (NeurIPS), vol. 33, pp. 1877–1901 (2020)
5. Cámara, J., Troya, J., Burgueño, L., Vallecillo, A.: On the assessment of generative AI in modeling tasks: an experience report with ChatGPT and UML. Softw. Syst. Model. **22**(3), 781–793 (2023). https://doi.org/10.1007/s10270-023-01105-5
6. Dziri, N., Lu, X., Sclar, M., et al.: Faith and fate: limits of transformers on compositionality. In: Advances in Neural Information Processing Systems (NeurIPS), vol. 36 (2023). https://arxiv.org/abs/2305.18654
7. Fill, H.G., Fettke, P., Köpke, J.: Conceptual modeling and large language models: impressions from first experiments with ChatGPT. Enterprise Modelling and Information Systems Architectures, vol. 18, pp. 1–15 (2023). https://doi.org/10.18417/emisa.18.3
8. Grattafiori, A.: The Llama 3 herd of models. arXiv preprint arXiv:2407.21783 (2024)
9. Härer, F.: Conceptual model interpreter for large language models. arXiv preprint arXiv:2311.07605 (2023)
10. Hendrycks, D., Burns, C., Chen, A., Ball, S.: CUAD: an expert-annotated NLP dataset for legal contract review. In: Advances in Neural Information Processing Systems (NeurIPS) Datasets and Benchmarks Track (2021)
11. Huang, L., Yu, W., Ma, W., et al.: A survey on hallucination in large language models: principles, taxonomy, challenges, and open questions. ACM Trans. Inf. Syst. **43**(2), 1–55 (2025). https://doi.org/10.1145/3703155
12. Jiang, A.Q., Sablayrolles, A., Mensch, A.: Mistral 7B. arXiv preprint arXiv:2310.06825 (2023)
13. Knuth, D.E.: Claude's cycles. Stanford University (2026). https://www-cs-faculty.stanford.edu/~knuth/papers/claude-cycles.pdf
14. Li, Y., Choi, D., Chung, J., et al.: Competition-level code generation with AlphaCode. Science **378**(6624), 1092–1097 (2022)
15. Mercado, J.S., Ma, Q., Cabot, J., Kelsen, P., Proper, H.A.: Towards human-in-the-loop LLM-enabled domain modeling. In: Bork, D., Lukyanenko, R., Sadiq, S., Bellatreche, L., Pastor, O. (eds.) Conceptual Modeling – ER 2025. Lecture Notes in Computer Science, vol. 16189, pp. 127–145. Springer (2025). https://doi.org/10.1007/978-3-032-08623-5_7

16. Mylopoulos, J.: Conceptual modelling, databases, and CASE: an integrated view of information systems development. In: Loucopoulos, P., Zicari, R. (eds.) Conceptual modelling and Telos, pp. 49–68. Wiley (1992)
17. Olivé, A.: Conceptual Modeling of Information Systems. Springer (2007)
18. Ouyang, S., Zhang, J.M., Harman, M., Wang, M.: LLM is like a box of chocolates: the non-determinism of ChatGPT in code generation. arXiv preprint arXiv:2308.02828 (2023)
19. Romera-Paredes, B., Barekatain, M., Novikov, A., et al.: Mathematical discoveries from program search with large language models. Nature **625**, 468–475 (2024). https://doi.org/10.1038/s41586-023-06924-6
20. Storey, V.C., et al.: Large language models for conceptual modeling: assessment and application potential. Data Knowl. Eng. **160**, 102480 (2025). https://doi.org/10.1016/J.DATAK.2025.102480
21. Wand, Y., Weber, R.: On the ontological expressiveness of information systems analysis and design grammars. Inf. Syst. J. **3**(4), 217–237 (1993)

From Text to Knowledge: An Ontology-Aware Triple Extraction Framework with LLMs

Marco Calautti[2], Damiano Duranti[1(✉)], and Paolo Giorgini[1]

[1] University of Trento, Trento, Italy
{damiano.duranti,paolo.giorgini}@unitn.it, damiano.duranti@gmail.com
[2] University of Milan, Milan, Italy
marco.calautti@unimi.it

Abstract. Constructing knowledge graphs from text while preserving compliance with a conceptual schema remains a key challenge in conceptual modeling. Although LLMs can extract entities and relations effectively, their outputs often violate ontology constraints, limiting their use in schema-driven systems. We propose an ontology-aware approach that treats the schema as a first-class input and combines schema-conditioned extraction with iterative refinement. In this process, violations of ontology constraints are translated into explicit feedback that guides subsequent generations. Experiments on a Wikidata-derived benchmark show that ontology-guided refinement significantly improves both schema compliance and overall extraction quality, enabling a compact 14B model under refinement to surpass a frontier model under single-pass extraction. Results generalize to anonymized data, indicating gains from structural reasoning rather than memorization. Our findings highlight the role of conceptual schemas as active drivers of LLM-based knowledge graph construction.

1 Introduction

Knowledge graphs (KGs) are a central abstraction for representing structured knowledge extracted from unstructured text. From a conceptual modeling perspective, a KG can be understood as the instance-level realization of an underlying *conceptual schema*, typically formalized as an ontology that specifies admissible classes, predicates, and integrity constraints such as domain and range restrictions. Ensuring that extracted knowledge complies with such a schema is not merely a syntactic requirement, but a fundamental prerequisite for enabling reasoning, data integration, and quality assurance in data-centric systems.

The problem of constructing a KG from text is therefore inherently tied to the problem of preserving schema compliance. However, despite decades of research in triple extraction—including rule-based, parse-based, and neural approaches—existing methods generally treat the schema either as a post-hoc validation layer or as implicit knowledge encoded within the model. This limitation becomes

P. Fettke et al. (Eds.): ER 2026, LNCS 17125, pp. 75–90, 2027.
https://doi.org/10.1007/978-3-032-40377-3_5

particularly evident in the era of Large Language Models (LLMs). Models such as Gemma [7], Qwen [14], LLaMA [8], and GPT [11] are highly effective at generating semantically rich triples, but their outputs often violate the constraints imposed by a target ontology. Typical issues include the misuse of predicates outside their declared domain or range, incorrect type assignments, and the introduction of semantically plausible but schema-incompatible relations. These limitations highlight a broader gap between generative AI and conceptual modeling: current LLM-based approaches do not explicitly integrate the conceptual schema as a guiding component of the generation process. As a result, the produced knowledge graphs are difficult to align with schema-driven systems where correctness is defined not only by semantic plausibility, but also by formal consistency.

In this work, we address this gap by treating the ontology as a *first-class* input to the extraction process. We propose an ontology-aware pipeline that combines (i) a schema-conditioned single-pass extraction step, and (ii) an *iterative, ontology-guided refinement* procedure. In the refinement phase, violations of ontology constraints are detected and translated into explicit natural-language feedback, which is then incorporated into subsequent prompts. This allows the model to progressively converge toward a knowledge graph that is both semantically faithful to the input text and compliant with the conceptual schema. Crucially, the refinement signal is *symbolic and explicit*, as it is derived from formal violations of domain and range constraints, rather than from scalar rewards or self-generated critiques. We evaluate our approach on a benchmark derived from Wikidata and on an anonymized variant designed to mitigate memorization effects, using five LLMs spanning a wide range of scales, from compact open-weights models to a frontier closed-source one. The results support three main findings: (i) ontology-guided iterative refinement substantially improves both schema compliance and overall F1-score across all models; (ii) compact open-weights models, when combined with the proposed refinement strategy, exceed the single-pass performance of much larger closed-source models, although the gap to those models under refinement does not close; and (iii) these improvements generalize to anonymized data, suggesting that they stem from structural reasoning rather than memorized knowledge. Overall, our results indicate that conceptual schemas should not be treated as passive validation artifacts, but as active drivers of the extraction process, opening new directions for integrating conceptual modeling principles into LLM-based knowledge graph construction.

The remainder of the paper is organized as follows. Section 2 reviews related work on triple extraction, LLM-based knowledge graph construction, and feedback-driven generation. Section 3 formalizes the problem and presents our ontology-aware methodology, including the single-pass extraction procedure, the iterative refinement loop, and the schema-derived feedback mechanism. Section 4 describes the benchmark, the ontology construction process, the anonymized dataset, and the LLMs used in the evaluation. Section 5 defines the evaluation metrics and reports the experimental results. Section 6 discusses residual error modes, methodological choices, limitations, and practical implications. Finally, Sect. 7 concludes the paper and outlines future research directions.

2 Related Work

KG construction from unstructured text has a long history in conceptual modeling, knowledge representation, and natural language processing. We organize prior work along three dimensions that are most relevant to our contribution: classical and neural triple extraction, LLM-based extraction, and iterative or feedback-driven generation strategies.

Classical and Neural Triple Extraction. Early Open Information Extraction (OpenIE) systems such as TextRunner [15] and ReVerb [6] relied on rule-based pattern matching, which limited generalizability. Subsequent approaches improved accuracy by exploiting syntactic analysis, but remained dependent on parser quality. Neural methods further advanced the field: Neural OpenIE [4] introduced encoder–decoder frameworks that avoid hand-crafted patterns, while end-to-end architectures such as REBEL [2] achieve state-of-the-art results but require extensive annotated datasets and significant computational resources. Crucially, none of these methods enforce *a priori* compliance with a given conceptual schema: schema constraints, when present, are typically applied as a post-hoc filter.

LLM-Based Extraction. LLMs such as GPT, Gemma, and Qwen have opened novel opportunities for triple extraction in zero- and few-shot regimes. Papaluca et al. [12] introduce knowledge-base context prompting but lack explicit schema enforcement and rely heavily on context quality. Zhang and Soh [16] propose "Extract-Define-Canonicalize", focusing on schema generation and canonicalization rather than on compliance with a pre-existing ontology. Text2KGBench [10] highlights the difficulty LLMs face in adhering to ontology constraints. Other approaches apply the ontology only as a post-hoc filter [3], preventing recovery from violations, or explore alternative extraction strategies without explicit schema integration.

Iterative and Feedback-Driven Generation. A separate line of work studies iterative refinement and structured reasoning for LLMs more broadly. Graph of Thought [1] and Self-Refine [9] introduce iterative reasoning and self-correction strategies, but these methods typically rely on *scalar* feedback or *self-generated* critiques. Our approach differs in a fundamental way: refinement is driven by *explicit, symbolic* feedback derived from formal ontology violations, with no reliance on the model's own ability to judge correctness. This makes the feedback loop both verifiable and aligned with the conceptual schema by construction.

Positioning. With respect to all of the above, our method uniquely combines ontology-aware prompting, iterative refinement driven by symbolic schema-derived feedback, and a systematic comparison across LLM scales on both natural and anonymized data. The resulting evidence, namely that a compact 14B open-weights model paired with schema-derived feedback exceeds the single-pass quality of a frontier closed-source model while producing schema-consistent triples, is, we believe, of particular interest to the conceptual modeling community.

3 Problem Description and Methodology

This section formalizes the problem of ontology-aware knowledge graph construction from text and presents our proposed methodology. We first introduce the formal setting, defining ontologies and knowledge graphs, and then describe our extraction approach. In particular, we present both a single-pass extraction strategy and an iterative refinement procedure, in which ontology constraints are used to guide the generation process through explicit feedback.

3.1 Preliminaries: Ontologies and Knowledge Graphs

Our goal is to transform unstructured text into knowledge graphs that capture its informational content while complying with a pre-defined conceptual schema, expressed here as an *ontology*. We start by fixing notation and terminology.

Ontologies. We assume infinite, disjoint, and countable sets C and P of *classes* and *predicates*, respectively. An *ontology* is a tuple $\mathcal{O} = (S, P, V, \mathcal{D}, \mathcal{R})$, where $S \subseteq \mathsf{C}$ is a finite set of *subject types*, $P \subseteq \mathsf{P}$ a finite set of *predicates*, $V \subseteq \mathsf{C}$ a finite set of *value types*, and $\mathcal{D} : P \to 2^S \setminus \{\emptyset\}$ and $\mathcal{R} : P \to 2^V \setminus \{\emptyset\}$ are functions specifying, for each predicate $p \in P$, the *domain* (resp., *range*) of p, i.e., the set of classes in S (resp., V) to which a subject (resp., object) of p can belong. Note that S and V may share classes.

Knowledge Graphs. We consider two kinds of triples. An *instance-of* triple is an expression $(s, \mathsf{instanceof}, c)$, where s is a string and $c \in \mathsf{C}$, stating that s is a member of the class c (e.g., *(Albert Einstein, instance of, Human)*). A *relationship* triple is an expression (s_1, p, s_2), where s_1, s_2 are strings and $p \in \mathsf{P}$, stating that s_1 is related to s_2 via p (e.g., *(Albert Einstein, place of birth, Ulm)*). For brevity, we may write $c(s)$ for $(s, \mathsf{instanceof}, c)$ and $p(s_1, s_2)$ for (s_1, p, s_2). A *knowledge graph* $\mathcal{G}$ is a finite set of triples. We say that $\mathcal{G}$ *complies with* $\mathcal{O} = (S, P, V, \mathcal{D}, \mathcal{R})$ iff: (i) for each instance-of triple $c(s) \in \mathcal{G}$, $c \in S$; (ii) for each relationship triple $p(s_1, s_2) \in \mathcal{G}$, $p \in P$; and (iii) for each $p \in P$, if $\mathcal{G}$ contains a relationship triple $p(s_1, s_2)$, then every instance-of triple $c(s_1)$ (resp., $c(s_2)$) in $\mathcal{G}$ satisfies $c \in \mathcal{D}(p)$ (resp., $c \in \mathcal{R}(p)$). Together, instance-of triples (which anchor entities to ontology classes) and relationship triples (which specify ontology-defined relations between entities) form the basic building blocks of our knowledge graphs.

3.2 Ontology-Aware Knowledge Graph Extraction from Text

Our goal is to construct, starting from a given text T in natural language, and an ontology $\mathcal{O}$, a knowledge graph $\mathcal{G}$ such that (i) $\mathcal{G}$ encodes the semantic information stored in T, and (ii) $\mathcal{G}$ complies with $\mathcal{O}$. Regarding (i), coming up with a formal definition of how well $\mathcal{G}$ encodes the semantic information in T is quite challenging, and thus property (i) will be experimentally verified by comparing the constructed knowledge graph with a reference one that has been manually constructed starting from the given text T. Regarding property (ii), since the process of extracting a knowledge graph from text is not precise, and prone to errors, guaranteeing full compliance with an ontology is unrealistic in practice. Hence, we aim to extract knowledge graphs with as few errors as possible w.r.t. $\mathcal{O}$. We will define what we mean by errors in a knowledge graph $\mathcal{G}$ w.r.t. an ontology $\mathcal{O}$ later in this section. Clearly, if the constructed graph $\mathcal{G}$ ends up having no errors w.r.t. $\mathcal{O}$, then $\mathcal{G}$ complies with $\mathcal{O}$.

We first start by discussing our approach at the high level, and then will go in further details regarding how we measure errors w.r.t. the ontology, and how we measure the general quality of the extracted graph by using the manually defined reference graph.

Consider some free-text T, and an ontology $\mathcal{O}$. We consider two strategies for constructing knowledge graphs from T that aim to comply as much as possible with $\mathcal{O}$. Both strategies employ an LLM M to produce sets of triples from T and $\mathcal{O}$:

- A *single-pass extraction* procedure, where the model M processes a single prompt embedding information regarding $\mathcal{O}$ and describing the task, and immediately outputs the desired triples.
- An *iterative, ontology-guided refinement* procedure, in which at each iteration, the generated knowledge graph is examined against the ontology $\mathcal{O}$. All errors in $\mathcal{G}$ w.r.t. $\mathcal{O}$ are collected, and then addressed in the subsequent iteration, where a new prompt is produced embedding not only $\mathcal{O}$ and the task description, but also all the errors that are present in $\mathcal{G}$.

We now discuss the above two approaches in more details.

3.3 Single-Pass Extraction

Under the single-pass approach, the model is fed with the input text T, a description of the ontology $\mathcal{O}$, and a prompt that specifies the required actions to take over T. In particular, the prompt asks the LLM M to perform the following:

1. Identify all relevant entities in the text and assign them to ontology classes.
2. Identify relationship triples (s_1, p, s_2) where $p \in \mathcal{O}$ and s_1, s_2 satisfy domain/range constraints.
3. Produce the output as a list of triples (s, p, o).

The model generates a set of triples in response to this prompt, without any follow-up queries or corrective steps. Although this approach is straightforward and efficient, it offers no mechanism for addressing the likely non-compliance of the resulting graph w.r.t. $\mathcal{O}$.

3.4 Iterative Ontology-Guided Refinement

In contrast to the single-pass extraction, this iterative procedure introduces a multi-round correction cycle. After obtaining a knowledge graph $\mathcal{G}$ from an initial execution of the single-pass approach discussed before, the iterative approach collects all the errors of $\mathcal{G}$ w.r.t. $\mathcal{O}$, and then it formulates a "correction prompt" highlighting these issues, and the LLM is asked to produce a new knowledge graph.

Errors Definition. Our approach considers the following two kinds of errors that might be present in a knowledge graph $\mathcal{G}$ w.r.t. an ontology $\mathcal{O} = (S, P, V, \mathcal{D}, \mathcal{R})$. An *instance of error in $\mathcal{G}$ w.r.t. $\mathcal{O}$* is an instance of triple $c(s) \in \mathcal{G}$ such that there exists a relationship triple of the form $p(s, s')$ (resp., $p(s', s)$) in $\mathcal{G}$ such that $c \notin \mathcal{D}(p)$ (resp., $c \notin \mathcal{R}(p)$). In other words, an instance of triple $c(s)$ is an error if it mentions an entity s which is declared to be an instance of a class c that does not appear as being part of the domain (resp., range) of a relationship triple $p(s_1, s_2)$ of $\mathcal{G}$ that mentions s as its subject (resp., object); we may say that $c(s)$ is an instance of error because of $p(s_1, s_2)$. A *relationship error in $\mathcal{G}$ w.r.t. $\mathcal{O}$* is a relationship triple $p(s_1, s_2) \in \mathcal{G}$, such that either $p \notin P$, or there is an instance of triple $c(s_1)$ or an instance of triple $c'(s_2)$ in $\mathcal{G}$ that is an instance of error because of $p(s_1, s_2)$.

How a Single Iteration Works. With the notion of instance of errors and relationship errors in place, we can now describe in details how our iterative ontology-aware approach is implemented. Assume T is the input text, and $\mathcal{O}$ is the ontology of interest.

1. The LLM first processes the prompt for the single-pass approach, constructed using T and $\mathcal{O}$.
2. Then, the generated knowledge graph $\mathcal{G}$ is used, together with $\mathcal{O}$, to collect all the instance of and relationship errors in $\mathcal{G}$ w.r.t. $\mathcal{O}$ in a set E. This step is performed by a deterministic procedure that directly evaluates the error conditions defined above over $\mathcal{G}$ and $\mathcal{O}$; the LLM plays no role in detecting violations, and receives only the resulting list E. Violation detection is therefore sound and complete w.r.t. the class of errors we define, and is not subject to the model's own judgment of correctness. Detection is currently restricted to *direct* domain and range constraints: subsumption reasoning over class hierarchies and richer constraint languages is left to future work.
3. A new prompt is produced that enumerates each error in E.
4. The LLM then returns a revisited knowledge graph $\mathcal{G}'$.

The above steps are repeated until a desired maximum number of iterations is reached.

3.5 Prompt Engineering and Error Feedback

To ensure reproducibility and clarify our methodology, we provide the exact structure of the prompts used in our pipeline.

Base Extraction Prompt. The initial single-pass extraction uses a prompt that dynamically integrates the ontology constraints. The template is as follows:

> *"Given the sentence [SENTENCE], Follow these steps: 1. Identify instances of classes mentioned in the information. 2. Create "instance of" triples for each identified instance. 3. Use only the properties explicitly mentioned in the information. 4. Ensure that the relationships you list are directly stated or can be unambiguously inferred from the information. 5. Use only the following exact properties: [PROPERTIES_LIST] 6. Apply properties only to instances that comply with the ontology constraints. 7. Validate that all relationships are consistent with the ontology. The response must be a list of complete triples with brackets in the form ['subject', 'property', 'object']... Provide a complete set of triples. Each triple must comply with the ontology constraints. Use only information from the sentence."*

The `[PROPERTIES_LIST]` is a dynamically generated string that lists each property along with its domain and range constraints (e.g., *"place of birth (Subject type: Human, Value type: City)"*).

Correction Prompt. When errors are detected (as defined in Sect. 3.4), they are compiled into a natural language list. The correction prompt is structured as follows:

> *"[BASE_PROMPT] Original Triples: [ORIGINAL_TRIPLES] Errors: [ERROR_LIST] Remember to follow all the guidelines mentioned in the base prompt, including using only the specified properties and ensuring all relationships are consistent with the ontology. Provide only the corrected set of triples."*

The `[ERROR_LIST]` explicitly states the violations, such as *"The triple (X, P, Y) violates the domain constraint of P (expected A, got B)"*. This direct feedback allows the LLM to understand specifically *why* a triple was rejected, rather than just being asked to "try again".

Stopping Criterion. The iterative process terminates as soon as any of the following conditions holds: (i) the constructed knowledge graph contains no ontology violations; (ii) the F1-score does not improve by more than 1% with respect to the previous iteration; or (iii) the F1-score decreases with respect to the previous iteration. Conditions (ii) and (iii) prevent the model from oscillating between equivalent fixes or "over-correcting" valid triples that the previous iteration had already produced.

3.6 Research Questions

With our two methodologies in place, our goal is to experimentally assess their validity, and in particular, address four primary research questions. These questions reflect the practical and theoretical interests in evaluating how LLMs can be implemented to produce high-quality, ontology-compliant knowledge graphs. In particular, we are interested in addressing the following questions.

1. **(RQ1): Model Performance Assessment**: How do different families of language models affect the performance of our ontology-aware extraction approach, particularly concerning the quality of the extracted graph?
2. **(RQ2): Ontological Consistency**: How many errors does the extracted knowledge graph contain w.r.t. the given ontology, in general, and how does this number impact the overall quality of the extracted knowledge graphs?
3. **(RQ3): Learning Efficiency**: How does the single-pass extraction approach compare to the iterative ontology-guided one, and can smaller language models achieve competitive performance over larger models, when they are employed in the iterative approach?
4. **(RQ4): Generalization Capability**: How well do both the single-pass and the iterative approaches work over data never seen by the underlying LLMs (i.e., anonymized data)?

In the rest of our paper, we will design a thorough experimental evaluation of our single-pass and iterative approaches in order to provide definite answers to the above key questions.

4 Benchmark

We start by discussing how the dataset used for our experimental evaluation is obtained, and which LLMs from the literature will be used for our analysis.

4.1 The Dataset

Our study employs a dataset originally developed in [13], which proposed an approach to map Wikidata statements to corresponding Wikipedia sentences. The dataset covers a set of subjects extracted from Wikidata. For each subject s, the dataset contains a collection C_s of pairs of the form $(T, \mathcal{G})$, where T is a short sentence in natural language stating some property of the subject s, such as “Ronaldo is a Football player”, and $\mathcal{G}$ is a set of triples describing *part* of the content of the sentence, such as (“Ronaldo”, $\mathsf{instanceof}$, “Football Player”).

Remark: We stress that the knowledge graph $\mathcal{G}$ attached to each text T does not necessarily cover all possible statements expressed in T. This means that although $\mathcal{G}$ provides a good basis for measuring the quality of the knowledge graphs extracted by our approaches, naive evaluation against $\mathcal{G}$ alone would underestimate the quality of our extracted graphs, since these may contain valid triples encoding statements present in the text but absent from $\mathcal{G}$. Unfortunately, we are not aware of other benchmarks which are as large as this one, that provides better quality ground truth graphs. We address this in Sect. 5 through tailored precision and recall definitions.

The dataset captures a wide variety of sentence constructions that reflect how the same factual content is linguistically expressed on Wikipedia. Since it includes ready-made pairs of sentences and Wikidata triples, it enables rigorous evaluations of extracted triples, without requiring users to perform an initial mapping themselves. Using these pre-associated sentences and triples, our experiments directly measure model performance in reconstructing Wikidata-style statements. This methodological choice allows our work to concentrate on ontology-aware prompting and evaluation metrics, rather than developing another manual or semi-automated alignment process. For the purpose of our experiments, we selected nearly 800 text-triple pairs from the overall collection, ensuring sufficient variety while keeping the corpus at a manageable scale.

To prepare this dataset for our specific experiments, we carried out several preprocessing steps that we discuss next.

- **Data Preprocessing.** We refined the dataset by removing extraneous metadata and merging sentences referring to the same subject into consolidated text blocks to capture richer context. Correspondingly, we consolidated the ground truth knowledge graphs, removing duplicate triples to ensure a consistent evaluation target.
- **Ontology Construction.** Since the dataset lacks explicit ontologies, we constructed them by querying Wikidata. For each subject, we retrieved all relevant predicates and their associated domain and range constraints (valid subject and object classes). This allowed us to build a precise ontology $\mathcal{O}$ for each text-graph pair, defining the valid schema for extraction.
- **Dataset Anonymization.** To mitigate potential bias from LLMs memorizing Wikipedia content, we created an anonymized version of the dataset. Entities were replaced with others of the same class (e.g., swapping "Einstein" with "Marie Curie" and "Ulm" with "Warsaw") while preserving sentence structure and semantic relationships. This ensures evaluation focuses on extraction capability rather than prior knowledge.

4.2 Models Coverage

In this section, we discuss the main large language models we use in our methodology. Recall that one of our research questions regards understanding how different LLMs compare w.r.t. the quality of the extracted graphs, and in particular, how smaller models behave against larger models, when they can gain help from our iterative ontology-aware approach.

In line with these objectives, we selected a diverse set of models in terms of size, architecture, and underlying training techniques. Specifically, we consider **GPT-4** [11], which is widely recognized as a leading large-scale (closed-source) model. **Gemma 2 9B** [7], which is a high-performance, yet compact model from Google. **LLaMA 3 8B** [8], an open-source model with a relatively smaller parameter count. **Qwen 2.5 7.5B** [14], which also balances smaller scales with competitive capabilities. **Qwen 2.5 14B**, which is a 14B variant of the previous model.

By comparing these models under both the single-pass approach and the iterative approach, we can evaluate the degree to which large-scale pre-training and vast knowledge influence triple extraction capabilities, as well as the extent to which smaller models can effectively close the gap through iterative refinement.

5 Experimental Evaluation

This section evaluates our two strategies for constructing knowledge graphs from free-text data, i.e., the single-pass approach, and the iterative approach, over the dataset discussed in Sect. 4.1, and by considering different language models among the ones identified in Sect. 4.2.

In order to properly measure the performance of the above approaches, we first need to introduce our key evaluation metrics.

Knowledge Graph Precision. At the high level, the goal of a precision measure is to quantify the percentage of correct objects produced by a system w.r.t. to the total number of objects produced by the system. In this sense, then, the precision of the extracted knowledge graph $\mathcal{G}$ should be the fraction of correct triples in $\mathcal{G}$. What we need to clarify is what we mean by "correct". As discussed in Sect. 4.1, recall that for each text T of our dataset, the corresponding ground truth knowledge graph $\mathcal{G}'$ contains only a partial encoding of all statements expressed in T. Hence, naively defining when a triple of the extracted graph $\mathcal{G}$ is correct simply as whether it appears in $\mathcal{G}'$ would, in most cases, let us conclude that $\mathcal{G}$ is of very low quality. Naive approaches to deal with this issue have been proposed in other works, such as [10], where a (relationship) triple is considered correct iff its predicate appears in the text T. We believe these approaches are too limited, and do not provide a sensible definition of when a triple in the extracted graph is meaningful or not. On the other hand, we cannot simply ignore the triples in the extracted graph $\mathcal{G}$ that do not appear in the ground truth, as this would lead to very high precision values.

For the above reasons, we believe that, although the ground truth $\mathcal{G}'$ could be used to define other performance metrics, as we are going to discuss later, it is not suitable for a proper definition of precision. Hence, we propose the following definition of precision that evaluates the quality of the extracted knowledge graph $\mathcal{G}$ exclusively on the basis of how compliant $\mathcal{G}$ is w.r.t. $\mathcal{O}$. That is, given the knowledge graph $\mathcal{G}$ obtained with one of our approaches from a given text T, and the corresponding ontology $\mathcal{O}$, the *knowledge graph precision of* $\mathcal{G}$ is the percentage of triples in $\mathcal{G}$ that are not errors w.r.t. $\mathcal{O}$, i.e., they are neither an instance of error, nor a relationship error (cf. Section 3 for the definition of errors).

Knowledge Graph Recall. We also need to provide a sensible definition of recall. A notion of recall should denote the percentage of expected objects that belong to the ground truth that are actually returned by the system. Again, since for a given text T, the ground truth $\mathcal{G}'$ does not encode all statements present in T. This means that by naively considering only the triples present in $\mathcal{G}'$, the above simple definition would very likely provide very high recall values, in most cases. Hence, we need a more refined notion of recall, in order to not incur in the above bias. In particular, our notion is the standard definition of recall, but evaluated over an extended version of the ground truth $\mathcal{G}'$ that contains additional triples that were not found in $\mathcal{G}'$.

In particular, we expand $\mathcal{G}'$ with a set of triples, denoted $I_{\mathcal{G}'}$, obtained exploiting once again the ontology $\mathcal{O}$. In particular, starting from the base set $\mathcal{G}'$ of triples in the ground truth, we can exploit the ontology $\mathcal{O}$ to derive new valid triples. In particular, new instance of triples derived from the relationship triples in $\mathcal{G}'$ that can be inferred using the domain and range constraint of the underlying predicate. Then, by considering the new graph $\mathcal{G}''$ obtained by adding to $\mathcal{G}'$ the set $I_{\mathcal{G}'}$, the *knowledge graph recall* of the knowledge graph $\mathcal{G}$ extracted from text T is the percentage of triples in $\mathcal{G}''$ that $\mathcal{G}$ mentions.

This approach allows us to measure the recall as a percentage of completeness, taking into account both explicitly stated relationships in the ground truth, as well as implicit ones.

Example 1. Consider an ontology containing the predicate placeofbirth with domain being the class Human, and range the class City. Given the text T containing the sentence "Albert Einstein was born in Ulm", and whose ground truth graph $\mathcal{G}'$ contains only the triple ("Albert Einstein", placeofbirth, "Ulm"), the extended version $\mathcal{G}''$ of $\mathcal{G}'$ will contain the triples ("Albert Einstein", placeofbirth, "Ulm"), ("Albert Einstein", instanceof, Human), and ("Ulm", instanceof, City). Then, if the extracted graph $\mathcal{G}$ mentions all the above 3 triples, then its recall is 1. If e.g., it mentions only two of these 3 triples, then its recall is 2/3.

This method of calculating recall provides a more comprehensive evaluation of our model's performance, accounting for both explicit and implicit information in the text, and ensuring that we capture the full semantic representation of the content.

Knowledge Graph F1-Score. With our notions of precision and recall in place, we can easily adapt the well-known notion of F1-score, by employing Knowledge Graph precision and knowledge graph recall. In particular, for a knowledge graph $\mathcal{G}$ produced by one of our approaches, starting from a text T and corresponding ontology $\mathcal{O}$, and assuming the corresponding ground truth knowledge graph is $\mathcal{G}'$, the F1-Score of $\mathcal{G}$ is computed as:

$$2 \cdot \frac{\text{Precision} \cdot \text{Recall}}{\text{Precision} + \text{Recall}},$$

where Precision is the knowledge graph precision of $\mathcal{G}$ and Recall is the knowledge graph recall of $\mathcal{G}$. The above notion of F1-score provides a single metric that takes both precision and recall into account, offering a balanced measure of the performance of our approaches.

5.1 Evaluation

We are now ready to evaluate both our single-pass and iterative approaches. Recall that in the single-pass approach, the chosen LLM is given a comprehensive prompt that specifies the required actions. In particular, as already anticipated in Sect. 3.6, it asks the model to identify all relevant entities in the text, assign them to relevant classes of the ontology of our dataset, and then identify all relationship triples ensuring they agree with the ontology constraints. Then, the model generates a knowledge graph in response to this prompt, without any follow-up queries or corrective steps. On the other hand, the iterative approach further refines the constructed knowledge graph $\mathcal{G}$ by pinpointing the errors in $\mathcal{G}$ by exploiting the ontology $\mathcal{O}$ and iteratively prompts the model to correct the errors. For each LLM M among the ones we discussed in Sect. 4.2, and for each text T coming from our dataset, and its anonymized version T', both our single-pass and iterative approaches were given as input T (resp., T'), and the ontology $\mathcal{O}$, and we let them construct a knowledge graph by using M as the underlying model; to select the number of iterations for the iterative approach, we used the F1-score as a reference, and we stopped according to the criterion defined in Sect. 3.5. Our findings are discussed in the rest of this section, and performance metrics are shown in Table 1, where we report for both approaches, the average precision, average recall, and F1-score, across all records (i.e., pairs of a text T and ontology $\mathcal{O}$) of both the main dataset, and the anonymized dataset.

The Effect of Anonymization. Table 1 shows that anonymization has limited impact on performance, with F1-scores remaining largely stable across datasets; the largest relative drop is 11.9% for Qwen14B under single-pass extraction and 5.7% under refinement. This is consistent with the models relying on structural understanding rather than on memorized Wikipedia facts (RQ4). We note, however, that our anonymization substitutes entities with other well-known entities of the same class, which perturbs the specific subject-object associations seen in training but does not remove the entities themselves from the models' prior knowledge; the result should therefore be read as evidence against reliance on memorized *statements* rather than as a full ablation of memorization.

Table 1. Average precision, average recall, and F1-score for the single-pass approach (left) and the iterative approach (right), over the main dataset (first number in a cell) and the anonymized dataset (second number in a cell).

LLM	Single-Pass			Iterative			
	Precision	Recall	F1-score	Precision	Recall	F1-score	Iterations
gemma9b	0.49/0.48	0.76/0.75	0.59/0.59	0.64/0.65	0.85/0.85	0.73/0.74	5
gpt	0.64/0.64	0.79/0.80	0.70/0.71	0.93/0.95	0.96/0.97	0.95/0.96	3
llama8b	0.34/0.34	0.61/0.61	0.44/0.44	0.53/0.55	0.69/0.70	0.60/0.62	5
qwen14b	0.57/0.49	0.80/0.75	0.67/0.59	0.83/0.77	0.91/0.88	0.87/0.82	7
qwen7b	0.26/0.24	0.71/0.73	0.38/0.36	0.41/0.40	0.72/0.76	0.52/0.53	5

The Single-Pass Approach

Table 1 reveals that single-pass extraction generally yields poor precision and only moderate recall, correlating with model size (GPT performs best but its precision and recall remain modest). The high error rate indicates that LLMs alone struggle with strict formal constraints (RQ1, RQ2).

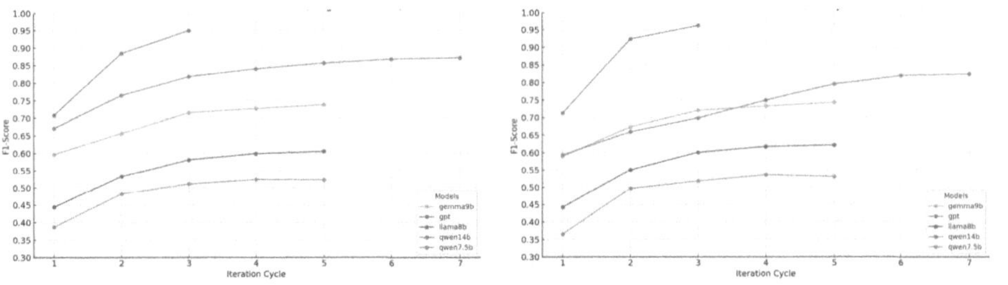

(a) Main dataset. (b) Anonymized dataset.

Fig. 1. F1-score across iterations for the main dataset (left) and anonymized dataset (right).

The Iterative Approach

We now move to analyze the performance of our iterative approach. In particular, as already discussed, we executed the iterative approach with a number of iterations that was guided by the stopping criterion of Sect. 3.5. We can see the result of this execution again in Table 1, which we also report graphically in Figs. 1a and 1b, for the main dataset and the anonymized dataset respectively. As we can see, the iterative approach indeed improves the overall performance, since it combines the great text-understanding capabilities of LLMs, with formal and precise knowledge of the underlying domain, which is something our experimental evaluation on the single-pass approach has shown the considered LLMs are not very good at dealing with. In particular, if we focus on the F1-score, and on the main dataset, we can see that the iterative approach provides 23.7%, 35.7%, 36.4%, 29.9%, and 36.8% increase in performance when considering gemma9b, gpt, llama8b, qwen14b, and qwen7.5b as the underlying LLM, respectively. Moreover, the number of iterations is quite limited, showing that with few iterations, the quality of the extracted knowledge graph can be improved considerably.

Crucially, Figs. 1a and 1b show that, on both datasets, while GPT-4 remains the strongest model overall, the much smaller Qwen 14B reaches competitive performance after 7 iterations. We note that the parameter count of GPT-4 has never been officially disclosed, and we therefore refrain from quantifying the scale gap. This is encouraging: it implies that high-quality, ontology-compliant knowledge graphs are reachable with much smaller and computationally cheaper models, provided that formal domain knowledge is injected in the form of explicit error feedback. With respect to RQ3, we conclude that the iterative approach yields substantial gains over the single-pass one, and that Qwen 14B under iterative refinement (F1 = 0.87) clearly surpasses GPT-4 under single-pass extraction (F1 = 0.70). We stress that the absolute gap to *iterative* GPT-4 does not close: it widens from 0.03 to 0.08 on the main dataset and from 0.12 to 0.14 on the anonymized one. The practical claim we support is therefore that refinement buys a compact model more than scale buys a frontier model in a single pass, not that the two become equivalent.

6 Discussion and Limitations

This section discusses the main implications of our results, focusing on the limitations of the proposed approach and their relevance from a conceptual modeling perspective. We analyze the types of errors that persist despite ontology-guided refinement, the assumptions underlying our experimental setting, and the broader role of conceptual schemas in guiding knowledge graph construction from text. We discuss these aspects in light of the research questions introduced in Sect. 3.6.

Residual Error Modes. While iterative refinement substantially reduces ontology violations (cf. precision in Table 1), two error patterns persist. First, occasional "hallucinated" properties remain: triples that are syntactically schema-compliant but not supported by the text. These are factual errors that schema-level feedback cannot detect by construction, since they do not violate structural constraints. Second, a small number of missing or incorrectly typed *instance-of* triples still occur, particularly for less common entity types. Schema feedback alone is therefore not sufficient: factual grounding and more robust entity typing remain open challenges. These findings relate to RQ2, showing that while ontology-guided refinement significantly reduces structural errors, certain classes of errors persist. From a conceptual modeling perspective, these limitations highlight a fundamental distinction between *structural correctness* and *semantic correctness*. While ontologies effectively constrain the admissible structure of knowledge graphs, they do not guarantee that extracted facts are supported by the source data. Bridging this gap requires integrating schema-level reasoning with grounding mechanisms, which we leave for future work.

Choice of Baselines. We deliberately do not include a "zero-shot, no-ontology" baseline. Such a baseline would generate triples whose predicates and types are drawn from the model's prior knowledge rather than the target ontology, and would therefore fail strict ontology-aware matching almost by construction, not because of poor extraction, but because of vocabulary mismatch. Our single-pass approach already provides a fair comparison, since it shares the same models and the same ontology, isolating the contribution of the refinement loop. This design choice allows us to clearly assess the impact of iterative refinement (RQ3).

Ontology Construction and Bias. The ontologies in our benchmark are obtained by querying Wikidata for predicates and constraints associated with each subject (Sect. 4.1). This corresponds to a "gold standard" setting in which the schema is assumed to be complete with respect to the relations expressed in the text, allowing us to isolate compliance capabilities from ontology incompleteness (RQ2). However, real-world conceptual schemas are often incomplete, evolving, or only partially aligned with the data. Understanding how ontology-aware extraction behaves under partial or noisy schemas is an important direction for future work.

Implications for Conceptual Modeling. Our results suggest that conceptual schemas can play a more active role in data extraction pipelines than traditionally assumed. Rather than serving only as validation artifacts, ontologies can be used to guide generation through explicit feedback, effectively acting as a form of *declarative supervision*. This opens the possibility of integrating schema design and data extraction more tightly, where conceptual models directly influence how knowledge is constructed from unstructured sources. These observations relate to RQ1 and RQ4, showing that ontology-aware refinement improves extraction quality across models and generalizes beyond memorized knowledge.

Entity Linking and Practical Implications. Triples are treated as string-based throughout: subjects and objects are surface forms rather than disambiguated identifiers, so our pipeline does not currently solve entity linking. The iterative refinement procedure is orthogonal to such an extension. From a practical standpoint, our key takeaway is that schema-driven refinement narrows the distance between compact open-weights models (e.g., 14B parameters) and frontier closed-source models without eliminating it, a useful property in conceptual modeling settings where data is sensitive, on-premise deployment is required, or the cost of frontier APIs is prohibitive. Moreover, this suggests that schema-driven approaches can reduce reliance on large-scale pretraining by injecting domain knowledge explicitly.

7 Conclusion

We presented an ontology-aware methodology for constructing knowledge graphs from text using large language models, in which the conceptual schema is treated as a first-class component of the extraction process. By translating ontology violations into explicit feedback, the proposed approach enables iterative refinement toward schema-compliant knowledge graphs. Our results show that schema-guided refinement substantially improves extraction quality and allows a compact 14B model under refinement to outperform a frontier model under single-pass extraction, while generalizing beyond memorized data. Overall, our findings highlight that conceptual schemas should not be treated merely as validation artifacts, but as active drivers of the generation process. This perspective opens new directions for integrating conceptual modeling principles into LLM-based data extraction. Future work includes extending the approach to richer ontology formalisms, incorporating entity linking, and evaluating additional models.

Supplemental Material Statement. The complete source code, datasets, ontology, and full experimental results are publicly available from Figshare [5], including the detailed results.

References

1. Besta, M., et al.: Graph of thoughts: solving elaborate problems with large language models. arXiv preprint arXiv:2308.09687 (2024)
2. Cabot, P.L.H., Navigli, R.: Rebel: relation extraction by end-to-end language generation. In: Findings of the Association for Computational Linguistics: EMNLP 2021, pp. 2370–2381 (2021). https://doi.org/10.18653/v1/2021.findings-emnlp.204
3. Chepurova, A., Kuratov, Y., Bulatov, A., Burtsev, M.: Prompt me one more time: a two-step knowledge extraction pipeline with ontology-based verification. In: Proceedings of TextGraphs-17: Graph-based Methods for Natural Language Processing, pp. 61–77. Association for Computational Linguistics, Bangkok, Thailand (2024). https://aclanthology.org/2024.textgraphs-1.5/
4. Cui, L., Wei, F., Zhou, M.: Neural open information extraction. In: Gurevych, I., Miyao, Y. (eds.) Proceedings of the 56th Annual Meeting of the Association for Computational Linguistics (Volume 2: Short Papers), pp. 407–413. Association for Computational Linguistics, Melbourne, Australia (2018). https://doi.org/10.18653/v1/P18-2065
5. Duranti, D.: Data and Implementation. Figshare (2026). https://doi.org/10.6084/m9.figshare.32297940
6. Fader, A., Soderland, S., Etzioni, O.: Identifying relations for open information extraction. In: Proceedings of the 2011 Conference on Empirical Methods in Natural Language Processing, pp. 1535–1545 (2011)
7. Gemma Team, et al.: Gemma 2: Improving open language models at a practical size (2024). https://doi.org/10.48550/arXiv.2408.00118
8. LLama team: The llama 3 herd of models (2024). https://doi.org/10.48550/arXiv.2407.21783
9. Madaan, A., et al.: Self-refine: iterative refinement with self-feedback. arXiv preprint arXiv:2303.17651 (2023)
10. Mihindukulasooriya, N., et al.: Text2kgbench: a benchmark for ontology-driven knowledge graph generation from text. In: Cheng, G., Li, J. (eds.) The Semantic Web - ISWC 2023, pp. 247–265 (2023)
11. OpenAI: GPT-4 technical report. arXiv (2024). https://doi.org/10.48550/arXiv.2303.08774
12. Papaluca, A., Krefl, D., Rodríguez Méndez, S., Lensky, A., Suominen, H.: Zero- and few-shots knowledge graph triplet extraction with large language models. In: Proceedings of the 1st Workshop on Knowledge Graphs and Large Language Models (KaLLM 2024), pp. 12–23. Association for Computational Linguistics (2024). https://doi.org/10.18653/v1/2024.kallm-1.2
13. Ta, H.T., Gelbukh, A.F., Sidorov, G.: Mapping process for the task: Wikidata statements to text as wikipedia sentences. arXiv (2022). https://doi.org/10.48550/arXiv.2210.12659
14. Yang, A., et al.: Qwen2.5 technical report (2025). https://doi.org/10.48550/arXiv.2407.10671
15. Yates, A., Banko, M., Broadhead, M., Cafarella, M., Etzioni, O., Soderland, S.: TextRunner: open information extraction on the web. In: Carpenter, B., Stent, A., Williams, J.D. (eds.) Proceedings of Human Language Technologies: The Annual Conference of the North American Chapter of the Association for Computational Linguistics (NAACL-HLT), pp. 25–26. Association for Computational Linguistics, Rochester, New York, USA (2007). https://aclanthology.org/N07-4013/
16. Zhang, B., Soh, H.: Extract, define, canonicalize: an LLM-based framework for knowledge graph construction (2024). https://arxiv.org/abs/2404.03868

Author Index

P. Fettke et al. (Eds.): ER 2026, LNCS 17125, p. 91, 2027.
https://doi.org/10.1007/978-3-032-40377-3

MIX
Papier aus verantwortungsvollen Quellen
Paper from responsible sources
FSC® C105338

If you have any concerns about our products,
you can contact us on
ProductSafety@springernature.com

In case Publisher is established outside the EU,
the EU authorized representative is:
Springer Nature Customer Service Center GmbH
Europaplatz 3, 69115 Heidelberg, Germany

Printed by Libri Plureos GmbH
in Hamburg, Germany